MY

SISTERS'

VOICES

MY SISTERS' VOICES

TEENAGE

GIRLS OF COLOR

SPEAK OUT

IRIS JACOB

AN OWL BOOK
HENRY HOLT AND COMPANY ~ NEW YORK

Henry Holt and Company, LLC

Publishers since 1866

115 West 18th Street

New York, New York 10011

Henry Holt ® is a registered trademark of Henry Holt and Company, LLC.

Library of Congress Cataloging-in-Publication Data

Jacob, Iris.

My sisters' voices : teenage girls of color speak out / Iris Jacob.—1st Owl Books ed.

p. cm.

"An Owl book."

ISBN 0-8050-6821-X (pbk.)

1. Teenage girls—United States.   2. Minority teenagers—United States.   I. Title.

HQ798 J32 2002

305.235—dc21   2002017203

Henry Holt books are available for special promotions and premiums.
For details contact: Director, Special Markets.

First Owl Books Edition 2002

Designed by Fearn Cutler de Vicq

Printed in the United States of America

1 3 5 7 9 10 8 6 4 2

For my mother

Contents

OURSELVES INSIDE AND OUT   138

RECLAIMING OUR VOICES 213

INTRODUCTION

Four years ago I read *Reviving Ophelia* by Mary Pipher. That book helped me understand myself and other teen girls. Pipher does a wonderful job of acknowledging teen girls and the hardships and the happinesses that we face. Her interwoven interviews, personal anecdotes, and facts made me realize what I was going through and that I was not alone.

Next I read Sara Shandler's book, *Ophelia Speaks*. Shandler wrote the book to give teenage girls the opportunity to tell their own stories. Because I was reading the stories in the girls' own words, I found it easier to connect to them and their stories and to really understand their meaning.

Reading both books profoundly helped my own search for self and my understanding of other girls. However, after reading and connecting to both, I felt something was missing. Pipher had discussed girls of color and so had Shandler. Yet I felt my struggle had not been truly identified. I felt as though girls of color had a unique and rarely validated struggle. I believed that in addition to bearing the weight of being teenagers and female, we also carry the enormous issues of race and ethnicity.

As I clarified my idea I began to think of ways to express it. My mother remembers that on the first day of 2000, I told her I wanted to write my own book, an *Ophelia Speaks* for girls of color. She said, "Do it," and I thought it was one of those ideas that would be quickly forgotten.

The idea stayed with me, though, because everywhere I looked, I began to see the need for such a book. Every time I heard racist comments, every time I noticed men putting down women, every time I saw girls of color in pain, I thought back to my idea. Every time I tried to bring about change and was told to back off, wait, or pick my battles, I thought about giving girls of color an opportunity to give their opinions, for once, instead of listening to everyone else's. Such a book wouldn't solve all the world's problems, I knew, but it could empower teenage girls of color. I wanted all the girls of color out there to be able to connect and to know that I feel what they feel. I wanted them to know that when they are stared at, mimicked, or harassed, they are not alone.

And so, with my mother's help, I found a wonderful agent and wrote a proposal. While doing research for the proposal I discovered that there were no self-help books on the market for teenage girls of color. Not one. This made me even more determined to see my project through. I felt as though we as girls of color not only deserved but needed a book, recognition, and a voice so we could be properly heard and acknowledged.

Within nine months of my original idea I had a book contract and went to work. I began to write letters to English teachers, clubs, organizations, and girls I knew to get pieces of writing. Again and again I heard from girls and women of color that the book was very much needed.

When the pieces began to arrive, I felt privileged to be able to read the innermost thoughts of these young women. The insights, feelings, and emotions these girls shared were captivating. The most impressive thing I found was that I could relate to every one. Their heartaches, loves, hates, laughter, and regrets were all something I have experienced in some way or another. My idea of connecting to other girls of color by speaking out and telling our stories had become a reality.

Working on this book began to occupy most of my spare time. When I would tell people about it, in the largely white community where I live, I would be met with blank stares. Then I would have to explain the concept and I would get more blank stares, or I would get patronizing comments like, "That's an interesting project." So I stopped telling anyone; even many of my closest friends had no idea what my book was all about. But then again, many of my close friends had never understood what I had experienced as a girl of color. I didn't tell them—for a variety of reasons—and they didn't ask.

Reading the submissions from girls ages twelve to nineteen, from all over the country, made me feel as though someone did, in fact, understand me. That's how I know this book is what I wanted it to be—and if the words on these pages comfort even one more girl of color, it will be a success in my eyes.

Many of the pieces of writing I received reminded me of my own experiences. I remember changing for gym class in sixth grade and having all the white girls stand and watch as I neatly pulled my braids back, so as to not mess up my hair by playing basketball. I remember the questions like: "Do you braid your hair every night?" and "Is that really human hair attached onto your hair or is it horse hair?" Such questions led me to hate myself and also my peers. I spent my middle school years hating all those who were around me. Because the city I lived in and the school I attended were more than 90 percent white, I had trouble finding anyone with experiences similar to my own.

In my sixth-grade year I made friends with a Latina girl named Rosa. Our friendship stemmed from our similar treatment by the whites at our school; we both dealt with the issues of identity, power, and culture. By eighth grade Rosa had been suspended four times and then switched schools. Her method of coping had been retaliating, telling the white people how she really felt. One day in the hall she told me she wanted to hit "this stupid lil' white girl." I told her to do what she wanted (I'll admit I wanted her to) and then she did. She grabbed the girl by her long blond hair, swung her around, and slapped her. Rosa's anger was not at this particular white girl. Her anger was within. She was furious that she was forced to be the translator between her parents and the rest of the city. She was angry that she had to continuously deal with the young white girls and their problems, which she felt were petty compared to her own.

Rosa and I took different paths. She let out her anger while I kept mine in. I wrote in my journal, cried, and treated everyone with contempt. I hated everyone and everything, yet I did not know why. I had three best friends; all were white. I was never actually close to them. We would share secrets, yet I never told them my most important one: that I was not like them. When race was brought up, one of us would quickly change the subject.

I know now that the anger Rosa and I experienced is not out of the ordinary. Teen girls of color all over the country feel this way! We are angry at not belonging. We are angry that society allows us to feel marginalized and oppressed because of our race and gender.

I hated that I was forced to sit in an all-white classroom and pray that the subject of race was never discussed. I was furious that I was regularly sexually harassed on the street, but that none of the boys in school seemed interested in me. I raged because while I knew I was beautiful, I felt so ugly.

When I was younger, my anger was turned inward. Something had to be wrong with me; it couldn't be anything else. I just didn't understand. I was convinced that I was alone because I had made myself that way. It was my fault that I was uncomfortable talking about race, no one else's. It was up to me to share my feelings—that's why no one talked to me about it, not because they didn't care, but because it was my problem. I had been told my entire life that I was beautiful and that I had outstanding potential, so it was my fault for not believing it.

As a result, I spent many nights screaming into my pillow and crying. At one point I came up with a new plan. When I would get angry, I would brush my hair. This way it would have a better chance of becoming straight (I assumed by some miracle that this would happen eventually), and I would have a great way of getting my anger out, brushing as hard as I could.

In eighth grade I became more involved in school. I spoke up, I organized a few clubs, and I became active in my community. Throughout this period I felt a sense of wanting to prove myself. I wanted the white kids at my school, the white people in the community, to know that I was capable of something. I wanted to impress them. For too long I had been quiet, and now they needed to know that I was capable. At the same time I realized that none of the white kids were doing this. I wondered why they didn't want to impress the community and feel like they needed to prove themselves.

In eighth grade I also made more friends and had more fun. However, my anger was still there. It was just cleverly masked and hidden. Now, instead of being angry at the white girls, I wanted to be like them. I dressed like them, I tried to have bangs, I shaved my legs (even though they contained almost no hair), and I wore makeup. But these behaviors were just ways for me to cope with my anger.

The next year my family moved away. I began to attend a small, predominately white school in a larger, more diverse city. That summer I once again became involved in my community. I attended a leadership institute on diversity work, worked at a camp for fourth- to sixth-graders, and went to a religious camp. It was then that I began to really change. I started to realize that I, as a teen girl of color, was different from others in society. I returned to my school the next year, and I focused on change. With much resistance, I was able to start affinity groups for girls and students of color. And this was when the idea of writing a book first came to me—not because I enjoy writing (although I'm learning to) but because I wanted to bring together girls of color.

To obtain submissions for the book I sent out thousands of letters to friends, English teachers, and organizations such as political groups and boys' and girls' clubs. With each letter I included a list of possible topics, ranging from racism to body image to family to abuse. I also put all the information about the book on a website, www.girlsofcolorwrite.com.

I did not receive any submissions on several topics I hoped to include, such as sexual orientation. I was disappointed that I also did not receive many submissions from some specific communities I had reached out to. It was necessary to obtain a signed release from each girl who submitted writing, and girls under eighteen had to have a parent's signature, so this might have discouraged some girls from opening their hearts. However, I am very grateful to all the girls, all over the country, who did take the time to write. Every girl wrote about what was closest to her heart, and that is reflected in these pages.

I asked every girl who submitted writing to include her age and racial/ethnic identity—as she defines it herself. I have not included the girls' hometowns, as I wanted to provide the contributors some degree of privacy. A few of the pieces were submitted by women who are no longer teenagers, but who wrote them when they were. In those instances I have used the author's age when she wrote the piece.

When I began working on the book, I had specific ideas about how I would arrange the contents. My ideas changed when I began receiving contributions. The sections in these pages reflect major themes in the lives of teenage girls of color. More Than Skin Deep is about racism and sexism and their effects. Our Roots examines our families, cultures, and traditions. The next section, Person to Person, focuses on our relationships with family members, friends, and lovers. Ourselves Inside and Out is about our search and struggle for identity in a world where teenage girls of color are held in low regard. Sharing Our Sorrows allows girls to share their stories of pain and loss. And, finally, Reclaiming Our Voices is a victorious celebration of empowerment.

All along, some people have misunderstood the purpose of this book. It is certainly not meant to exclude or promote discrimination

against white teenage girls. It is not meant to project negative atti-
tudes about anyone. This book is for teen girls of color to express
what they have for so long kept to themselves. It is meant to allow
teen girls to find a common bond and to be able to step away from
nurturing others and instead learn to nurture themselves. I have been
active in antiracism work, where affinity groups are common and
recognized as an important part of diversity. We gain strength
and support from people similar to ourselves. Just as in the 1960s
and 1970s, when women found that getting together in groups to
talk about their experiences was helpful, this book brings together
girls who share a common bond. Teenage girls of color as a group
need to support one another, care for one another, use our voices,
and most of all demand to be heard.

As I've worked to assemble the pieces of writing in this book, I've
laughed, cried, and had my breath taken away. Some of us are just out
of childhood; some of us are very nearly adults. Some of us come
from the poorest locales in the nation; some of us from very privileged backgrounds. Some of us are biracial or multiracial; some of us
are disabled; some of us are lesbians or bisexuals. We come from all
different ethnic, cultural, and spiritual traditions. We are immigrants, some of us. We are mothers, some of us. We are beauties,
inner and outer. We are heroines. We are winners, every one of us.
We are poets. We are the present. And, make no mistake, we are the
future.

MY

SISTERS'

VOICES

MORE THAN SKIN DEEP

I love my skin. I love the feeling, the texture, the heritage, and the warmth I feel when I look in the mirror and see this beauty encompassing me.

When I first decided to write this book, I was not completely sure if there would be a huge difference between sisters of color and white girls. Then I started receiving pieces. Many, many girls wrote about racism or skin color. I was amazed. I knew race was important to me, but to see it addressed and expressed by so many others was exhilarating.

In this section, girls write about personal experiences, about society, about the effects of race, ethnicity, and gender on our personalities and lives. I could not include nearly as many pieces as I would have liked, and I found it very difficult to know which ones to include. I tried to break down the pieces into categories such as "internalized feelings" or "racist comments" and then chose a representative piece from each category.

So all the pieces in More Than Skin Deep represent many others. We as sisters of color encounter one experience after another in which we are forced to focus on our skin and our gender and how we feel as a result of the experience.

In this section, we discuss, accept, embrace, celebrate, and go beyond our skin.

The summer before my junior year I met a girl named LaNisha at a diversity program. We stayed up late one night talking.

LaNisha shared with me her pain, her happiness, and her anger. One of the stories that most caught my attention concerned her job. She told me that every day she attended school, took a forty-minute bus ride to Taco Bell, and then worked the night shift. She spoke of how the white customers would make attempts not to touch her hands as they gave her the money for their food. With this she began to cry. She said once she looked a white person in the eyes and said, "So what, you think you gonna get a disease?" and was almost fired. LaNisha learned to keep her mouth shut despite her feelings. Every day she had to encounter the same thing and deal with the same emotions.

As we sat there that night I did not pretend to have experienced the same situation, but I did know the feeling. A feeling of being contaminated and dirty. A feeling of being not wanted solely based on my skin color. This is the feeling Simone describes in her piece "The Smoking Section."

THE SMOKING SECTION

Simone Senior, 17

BLACK

 "Do you see that?" She dumped a fresh pot of coffee into the sink.

"Yeah," I confirmed, pointing to the steam.

"Lady in table 51 thinks the coffee's too cold," Robyn vented, stomping her tiny feet to the coffee machine.

Sharing her frustration, I offered my advice. "Maybe you should spill it on her so she'll know how hot it is." We giggled, secretly wishing it was an option. Her airy chuckle faded as she headed for table 51 in the smoking section. My styrofoam cup of coffee in hand, I followed. I coiled myself in the corner of booth 61, across from 51, and watched Robyn take the rest of the lady's order. While pouring coffee, she allowed her hand to slip and steaming liquid trickled onto the lady's arm. "Oops," she cried. From the corner of her eye, Robyn glanced at my wide smile. I couldn't believe she'd done it. I never would have had the nerve. Then again, she was screwing the owner's son, so she could do damn near anything and not get fired.

Robyn hurried away, her cheeks almost popping with bottled-up laughter. The gray-haired lady turned to me and squinted her eyes. "Hi," I initiated. She curled her thin lips upside down and jerked her head around. Icy. I inspected her eyebrows for icicles but found none. Maybe I was just cold. I was often greeted with her same frosty attitude. But I felt warm, all scrunched up in the corner of booth 61, my black shoes digging deep into the blue plastic seat cushion. I figured IHOP was filled with cold people, people who outside of these walls had no definite place but felt at home among other outsiders. We all complained about our jobs. But we kept coming back. We knew it was the only place where a bunch of cold people could get together and feel heat.

The cook peeped his head through the kitchen window and excitedly waved his hand. The kitchen served as a divider between the nonsmoking and smoking section; however, it was closer to the smoking section. Remembering it was the quiet start of a stormy Sunday morning, I sunk deeper into the cushion. From where I sat, I could see the cook flip the last of the bacon. He poured a bucket of water on the grill to clean it. The grill's steam clouded the area where he stood. The kitchen's warmth flooded that air and thawed the chill in me.

Robyn plopped down into booth 61, across from me, the back of her head to the frigid lady. "Did you see that?" she whispered, her eyes bright with excitement.

"Yeah." I smiled.

I liked Robyn. I wanted to grab the bouncy blond hair that blossomed like a daffodil from her scrunchie. She was round—not fat but fluffy. I complimented her on her ability to fake happiness in the face of a cursing customer. Certainly, she entertained me. But we would never be friends. We were cordial, laughing and frowning when appropriate. But like all the waitresses, we had nothing in common except our IHOP applications. We had been pulled from our respective isolated walks of life and thrown into this deep pool. We only held on to one another to stay afloat. We bonded in a world that didn't exist beyond those glass doors. Outside we didn't know each other. We forgot any joy or sadness that may have flooded the IHOP air. But right now, in the smoking section, we were sisters.

"Whoooh," she pushed a whirlpool of air from her mouth. She tried to calm herself. Her pale white hand covered her lips as if to lock in extra giggles. "I can't wait to make my appointment." She stared off into space.

"What appointment?" I snapped her out of her daydream.

"My tanning appointment," she answered, rubbing her fingers over my hand, admiring my brown complexion.

"Isn't that bad for your skin?" I felt sorry for her. One day she'd be a prune.

"Yeah," she admitted. "But it feels so good. It's like you're in a tub of sun, heat soaking into every inch of your body." She released my hand and basked in the feeling she'd awakened. "I love it. I go every week." She didn't have to explain herself, anymore. I understood. Sometimes people do extreme things to feel warm.

By now, table 51 had been cleared and the gray-haired lady had been replaced by a middle-aged black woman. She stuffed her bulging gut into the booth. Robyn leaped from her seat to take the woman's order. Robyn stood, weight in her right hip, flipping page after page of her pad, scribbling sides and substitutions. The lady had cut and pasted the IHOP menu into an unrecognizable meal, which, once delivered to her, spanned the entire width of table 51. She had a T-bone, pancakes—chocolate chip and buttermilk—eggs scrambled with cheese, a side of bacon, a side of sausage, a side of ham, and coffee. And a Diet Coke. Before sticking her fork into her meat, she barked, "It ain't done."

"I beg your pardon." Robyn raised her arched eyebrows.

"I said well. Dis got blood on it." She shoved the plate at Robyn.

"Okay." She smiled. "I'll have him cook it some more."

Robyn returned with the burnt T-bone. The lady took a deep breath. "Dese eggs don't got enough cheese in 'em." She kept her head straight and stuck the plate in Robyn's face. Robyn's eyes met mine. We both grinned.

After running Robyn around the restaurant in search of extra butter, ketchup, hot sauce, and A. 1 sauce, the lady was set. She gobbled her greasy food like it was her last supper. "I hate that," Robyn exclaimed, draping the top of her body over table 61. We snickered. We understood the agony of an annoying customer. "I'm sick of this table," she whined. "Next time, you take it."

"Okay." I knew her feet were tired, and my butt was numb from sitting so long. She laid back in booth 61 and I stood, stretching.

The lady left a dollar tip. An old white man filled her space. He limped even with the aid of his cane. Once seated, he folded his *New Haven Register*. I tapped my pad on the back of his seat, waiting for him to finish his article. He gazed up at me. His bottom lip dropped. "Coffee," spilled from his mouth. He looked at me crossly as I left to fetch his pot of coffee. When I returned, he was gone. Robyn was lifting the menu from table 51.

"What happened?" I wondered, placing the coffeepot on the table.

She didn't look at me. "He forgot he had to go somewhere."

"What really happened, Robyn?" I lowered my eyes to hers.

Sadly looking into my face, she said, "He asked me to be his waitress."

She swallowed. Hard. "He said he didn't want a black person handling his food." Her words came like a flood. It drenched me, and I dropped into booth 61. "So, I told him he had to leave." She could've done whatever she wanted in that restaurant. She wouldn't have gotten fired if she took his order, if she allowed one more racist gesture to slip by unchecked. But without a second thought, she protected her fellow waitress. She sat next to me and looked me in my eyes. I was so alone. My eyes surveyed the restaurant, and I realized everyone was a million shades lighter than me. A chill came over me.

"I really should have smacked him," she tried to comfort me. Smack him. What would that do? How would that thaw his frozen heart? She was puzzled. She'd never have to feel this cold, never have her skin regarded as poison. My lips quivered. Tears welled up in my eyes. "Don't." Her arms enveloped me, spreading her body heat over my shivering bones. Of all the antics IHOP customers have pulled, this was the first for Robyn. She knew that it wouldn't be the last for me. We sat in booth 61, in the smoking section, in the tranquil waters of each other's warmth. Not drowning. Floating on one another. Reflected in my tears, she could see a world she never knew existed outside of the IHOP doors. I was her window with an ocean view. She was the raft that would take me back to dry hot sands.

When I first read Wendi's poem, I was a little stunned. I couldn't see how anyone would actually believe that they themselves were the problem and that they needed to change. I was also surprised because I'd met Wendi and saw her as a beautiful, strong young woman with high self-esteem.

I began to think about Wendi's words. I thought about how many times I'd felt that I was the problem or that everything would be better if I were to change. I remembered all of my friendships that would go bad once race had been brought up or how if I just could keep my mouth shut everything would be okay. I began to relate to Wendi's words and understand how she felt.

Too often, we as girls of color feel as though we should change to fit the norm. We follow our white peers, either out of fear of being ourselves or just because we change ourselves to be like them. I hope someday Wendi, myself, and the rest of us who feel this realize that we should not change ourselves but instead be our authentic selves as fully and as truly as we can.

THE BLACK SHEEP

Wendi Nevels, 16

BIRACIAL

I am the Black sheep in a herd shed with white
I do not flee, but I do not fight

Rebellion is brewing inside of my brain
So much this though I'm going insane

Sit back, Relax, Keep quiet, be still
So much these commands led on by my will

Inside this herd I stand alone
No family no friends no welcome my own

Forced into the realization that the problem I can't see . . .
I will not fight!
The problem is me

Taught to love and give
Power!
Taught also to fight and live

Fight or flee
Ultimatum?
This is not me

The leader has control of this herd shed with white
Giving them the ultimatum to flee or fight

Only accepted because of the paint
Yet the color so strong the fumes so faint

Forced into the realization that the problem I can't see.

I will not flee!
The problem is me

I don't know how many times I've seen the commercials that portray women as nothing more than sex objects. The beer commercials with women who are half dressed and loving the men who drink beer; the shampoo commercials with women who just love to shower all the time; and, of course, the lingerie commercials featuring women who love their new panty and bra set and can't wait to slowly, sexually, show it to the world.

These commercials not only are degrading to women but also are obviously not at all true. I have yet to know anyone who actually, while wearing nothing more than her underwear, dances slowly, for long periods of time, to seductive music, her hair blowing away from her pouting face.

While these images may not seem to be destructive, in many ways they are. When women are objectified in the media, they are in turn objectified in their everyday lives. Because of commercials, movies, magazines, and many other areas of mainstream society, both men and women absorb destructive images of female bodies, their sexuality, and their intelligence. If society is ever to eliminate the sexism that we as females of color encounter, we must challenge these blatantly sexist influences.

In her piece "My First Love: Skratching," Brooke critiques a particular TV commercial for failing to portray women with the same talent as their male counterparts.

MY FIRST LOVE: SKRATCHING

Brooke Wilson, 19

AFRICAN AMERICAN

Great American popular culture never ceases to amaze. The latest installment in my chronicles of female objectification, exploitation, and downright patronization comes courtesy of Gap Incorporated. It's a Friday night, and I have just finished another frustrating practice session on a set of turntables. I sit down to relax and watch some TV after those hours of hard work, only to find out in thirty seconds that it didn't really mean anything.

In those thirty seconds Gap Inc. shows three people, six turntables, and three mixers. Normally this equation would add up to three DJs, but somehow Gap's answer to this math dilemma is two DJs and one groupie. If you saw the ad, you know that the DJs are Rob Swift and Shortkut and the groupie is a female model/actress. If you've never seen the ad, you may be asking yourself, "How did Gap come up with that answer—it just doesn't add up!" Well, for those of you who haven't seen it, here's how they did it:

Step 1: Girl starts record.
Step 2: Girl watches and dances around as two boys skratch to record.
Step 3: Music stops and girl says to camera/world, "My first love . . . boys who skratch."

Reality is a strange and malleable thing, and this commercial would have the average person believe that in reality girls don't skratch or even DJ. Of course, in the beginning of the commercial it appears as though she at least starts the record even if that is the limit to her action.

However, my team of top-notch Gap ad analysts has discovered that the music starts even before the model takes her hand off the record, which leads us to the conclusion that she did not participate whatsoever in the music making and was, in fact, there only to wear the jeans and be looked at. You may now gasp in shock.

Let's not forget that she is there to watch and listen to the undeniably talented Swift and Shortkut tear it up on the wheels of steel. "Okay, but at least she's a fan of the music," you say. This might have been true had it not been for her admission at the end of the ad to loving boys who skratch. This makes it depressingly obvious that she is there not so much to listen to the music as she is to slip Shortkut or Swift her phone number. Believe me, she's not there for tips on beat juggling because she has already made it clear she couldn't care less about being a DJ. The model's first love is not skratching, not faders, not needles or turntables, not even skratch music, it's just boys who skratch. It would have been incredibly easy to take out the words "boys who skratch," and replace them with "skratching," which would have saved the entire commercial from the depths of stereotypical trash it sank to.

Sadder still is the fact that not only did Gap Inc. overlook this easy fix, they didn't even start with the logical step of casting a famous female DJ in place of the model. Yet again I know what you're thinking: "Yeah, what about Pam the Funkstress from the Coup! She's famous and she would have been good!" But Pam the Funkstress wasn't in the ad because Pam isn't a model. Not only does she not fit the skinny white mold demanded of most models, she actually has cultivated a talent. Having a profession and a talent for something other than applying makeup aren't very helpful when all you should be thinking about are boys and jeans.

Darting back and forth between taking the ad seriously and seeing it as just another cultural faux pas brought to you by Gap Inc., I can't decide what to make of it. Granted, there are a lot of DJ groupies out there who instead of getting dreams or hobbies of their own, latch themselves on to a man and his dreams. But more importantly there are a whole lot of girls who DJ.

I finally decided that I would be doing a disservice to all of the female DJs out there if I didn't take it seriously. After all, Gap Inc. seems to have gone out of its way to insult my intelligence in an attempt to replace the ambitions of girls who want to DJ, play a sport, write a book, or make a movie, with the desire to find a boy who does something great and bask in his ambitions. It's not as if this is forty years ago and the instinct for women to seek out a provider is still necessary. Women in America are able to provide for themselves and create their own lives on their own terms. The question is, why would the Gap promote this pathetic dependent lifestyle?

Just ask yourself: Is Gap selling jeans? Yes. Lifestyle ideals through fashion? Most likely. An ideology? Unfortunately. As usual corporate America has taken the worst aspect of a culture (groupies) and marketed it as the respectable norm, totally ignoring the amazing but true fact that girls DJ and sometimes wear jeans at the same time.

In the middle of my sophomore year, my high school drama department had a clothing sale. All the costumes used in past performances were on sale. A black friend of mine purchased an Asian-styled robe that had been used in the performance of The King and I. *When I asked her what she was going to use it for, she replied she would probably wear it around the house or when she went out.*

I felt very uncomfortable about this, but wasn't sure how to explain this feeling to my friend. I then thought of my friend's own connection to African culture and wearing Kente cloth. I found what she was doing—purchasing and wearing Asian cultural clothing—very similar to white people purchasing African clothing, instruments, and so on, and wearing or displaying them as if they were their own. We agreed that this felt insulting, almost as if our culture was stolen, mocked, or belittled. So often I feel that white Americans have appropriated the cultural characteristics of people of color and thus given us the impression that it is okay for us to do so as well. It's important for us, as people of color, to remember to honor all cultures.

In her piece "A Culture of Our Own," Vannah speaks of how she feels as a black female when her culture is taken away and manipulated by white people.

A CULTURE OF OUR OWN

Vannah Shaw, 15
BLACK

Many times I have been criticized for the way I am. Either someone will say, "Why do you talk so ghetto?" or in language class I get an answer wrong because I am used to saying a phrase the "wrong way" (using incorrect English). For once I would like someone to embrace me the way I am, to talk to me for me. For once I would like to be able to write a paper and be able to put it in my own words and phrases without my teacher telling me to change it. Or for once I would like to watch a TV show with black people that doesn't suggest that we are just comics, or a commercial that doesn't imply that all we do is sing. While humor and song lift the spirit, which is a big part of my culture, I would like to be taken seriously.

As you probably have figured out I am talking about stereotypes that are usually associated with African Americans. One thing I don't like is the criticism I get for using Ebonics, which is also associated with African Americans. This is what I speak and what I am used to hearing. As you also know, this type of talk is not always accepted. If you go on a job interview, talking about "Wassup mayne, can you hook a brother/sister up?" would get you laughed at and dismissed. I am 99.9 percent sure they would not be calling you back. Or even when I am talking to an adult, and bust words like "floss" or "wodie," they start acting "drove" (crazy).

I don't think just because you are around a certain type of people, you have to change your vocabulary. But in certain situations, you should just keep it professional. Some African Americans aren't well educated, but you have that in every culture.

When I am talking to Caucasians that are not "black at heart" and I start saying things like "sho' ya right," they look at me like I'm crazy and laugh. But in about five years they will start saying it, too. One example is "the bomb." I started saying that in the third grade, but six years later it's become a "teen word," what the kids are saying now.

Another linguistic thing that African Americans are pinned to that is also looked down upon is rap. Since the music "crossed over," and Eminem joined the Dr. Dre clique, all I've heard is, "Will the real Slim Shady please stand up?" Also, stations play his songs even if they play no other rap music. To me, this is Elvis all over again. A white man steals African American music and gets paid for our work.

An additional thing that I have noted is how white people and black people view cultures. If you go to a mixed school, I am almost sure you had the conversation about slavery. To them it's over and done with, and we should just drop our culture so that everyone is called American. Not to look over anyone else's culture, but why should we lose what little African pride we have so that we can all be one? Then, why do they make such comments as, "Everything is okay, and we are all equal"? Most of them have never been harassed by police just because of their color. They don't have to worry about what school they are going to if the desegregation program ends. Most of them think everything is right with the world, and the discrimination described by African Americans is exaggerated. Which most times it is not.

White people also ask us silly questions that make no sense, such as, "Why do you guys give shout outs on TV?" Another person asked me a while ago, "Why did a lot of black girls start getting twisties, now everyone wears them." The number one thing that irks me is that to them, everything that is messed up or not quite right is

"ghetto," and then they want to call me "ghetto." Or are they imply-
ing that something is wrong with me? I hope not!

We are in America, which is known as the most racist country in
the world. Even as a child I could sense some of the racial prejudices
around me. Not to say that it is all white people, and I'm sure I could
be a little more understanding in some areas pertaining to them as
well. The only thing is that as a minority, it affects me a little more.

In conclusion, I would like to say that I like white people. They
know this because I interact with them every day and it's real. It's just
that one day I wish poems about how my people as a minority needing
to survive will no longer need to be written. I wish that one day, my
people will not have to teach their children how to act around whites.
I wish that one day I will not be associated with poverty, but as the
future, as tomorrow. And I wish that one day, we can just be people.

*My senior year of high school started off a little strangely. A few friends of
mine thought it would be hilarious to nominate me for homecoming queen. I
thought it would also be funny, simply because so many girls wanted to be
homecoming queen while I really had no interest in it.*

*The day came when we had the pep assembly to announce the nominees. I
looked around at the huge senior class that I was now part of and decided the
joke would go way too far if I were actually to be nominated. But when the
names were read, sure enough, mine was one of them. I went to the stage, bowed
for my friends, and stood with the other nominees. After the ceremony I heard
rumors that a number of girls were angry with me. They thought I should not
have been nominated because I didn't deserve it and didn't want it badly
enough.*

*The following weeks were most enlightening. I was treated differently by
my peers, and even by the administration; it was as though I were suddenly one*

of the really popular people. I went to rehearsals where I learned how to walk for the coronation, posed for dozens of photographs, and was required to spend a lot of time thinking about my appearance.

When the night finally came, I was fed up with the entire process. I had always hated the idea of homecoming royalty and what it represented—a beauty and popularity contest—and now I had an insider's view, which was even more negative. My dress for the coronation was red, and in order to enjoy the situation a little more, I decided to wear a red wig to match. I stood on stage with the other nominees for queen—all white, slender, pretty girls, some of whom were very nice and smart, but all of whom had spent hundreds of dollars on outfits, makeup, nails, and hairstyles. I felt like an imposter and was thankful that I did not win.

Afterward, I was relieved but somewhat horrified that I had actually participated in the event. But then I thought about what a black student had said to me a few days before. She told me she was so glad I had been nominated and that she and all her friends would definitely vote for me. I began to think about how my nomination had affected the other girls of color in the school. For the first time in I don't know how long, a girl of color had actually been nominated for homecoming. This gave all of the other girls a new feeling of hope and encouragement that they, too, could be seen as attractive and popular by other students. I realized that I was not only representing myself and the joke my friends played, but I was also representing every girl of color at my school. Although I was still upset with the nature of the contest, I was glad I had taken part in it—not for the school's sake but for all the girls like me.

In "Standards of Beauty," Nzinga tells of the beauty contest she took part in and how she as a black female felt. Nzinga and I approached the contests we were in differently than many white teen girls would. We were representing a people, not just ourselves.

STANDARDS OF BEAUTY

Nzinga Moore, 19

BLACK

I recently read an article about a Ugandan woman rejected from the Face of Africa beauty contest because her hips were too big . . . by half an inch.

The story of the woman in Uganda made me think about my first beauty pageant—just a few months ago. It started when I was sitting in my normal place of study, on campus, and I picked up our school's newspaper. Flipping through to the classified section, I ran across an ad that read, "Earn up to $10,000 in scholarship money." The ad was for a local scholarship pageant.

That night I went home and checked the pageant's website. But as I scrolled down the page, I found that the application deadline had passed. Instead of giving up hope, I searched the Internet until I found another local pageant. It was for the title of Miss Contra Costa and Miss Greater East Bay 2001. I entered my information and requested an application.

A couple of weeks later I found myself driving up a hill on a narrow curvy road, past beautiful homes with white picket fences. As I slowly pulled into the driveway butterflies in my stomach began to flutter and I started to question myself. "Are you sure you want to do this?" I asked myself. I parked the car and stepped out. "Yes," I said, as though to reaffirm my decision. "Yes."

An older Caucasian woman, small and petite, opened the door and greeted me with smiles of enthusiasm. But the faces of the girls on the other side of the door were different. As soon as I stepped inside I felt as if their eyes were peering through me and they were ranking me on the "how likely is she to win" scale. I was not nervous because I had walked into a room full of strangers. I was nervous because the room was filled with girls who looked nothing like me, yet we were all going to be judged by the same standards. But would these standards include what I embody, the diaspora of the African?

I have always competed with people of different races for grades, jobs, and sports, but somehow when it came to beauty, it was really uncomfortable. I became convinced it was more than just a competition of beauty. I really wanted the winner to be African American. And I wanted it to be me.

In the end, after the swimsuit competition and all, I was second runner-up. I got some flowers and scholarship money. But the two girls who ranked above me were tall, shapely blondes. So I'm left with the question—what are the standards of beauty? And are we really any different—me, earning second prize, and the woman from Uganda, who never even made the first cut?

In the next piece, Nneka, a Nigerian immigrant, talks about breaking down stereotypes. After I read Nneka's piece I let my mother read it. She commented on how awesome it was that Nneka felt such a strong passion about changing the way others thought. She talked about how, when she was a single mother raising a black child, many people made assumptions about both of us, and how she loved to prove them wrong. And she reminded me that proving stereotypes wrong is a common theme in my family.

I try every day to challenge some kind of stereotype, whether it is one that affects me or others. I love to change people's minds and see them learn to accept others. I believe everyone can relate to Nneka's piece, as we are all stereotyped in one way or another.

FEAR

Nneka Nnaoke Ufere, 14
NIGERIAN

Being Nigerian, I have never really understood the whole idea of racism and discrimination. One could argue that this is because Nigeria is one of the few countries that have blacks in the majority (one out of every five Africans is Nigerian), but I actually believe that there is a very different cultural mentality there than here in the United States.

My parents acknowledged this and have been making sure that my brothers and I remember our true heritage. In this country where all people are declared equal by law there is still an underlying rejection and fear of people of color. For us not to consider ourselves inferior we have to connect to our own culture. My parents believe that this will give us the pride and strength needed to face adversity and overcome any obstacles.

But sometimes I really wonder if the people causing all of the discrimination are really thinking rationally. Why are some people so afraid of me, a fourteen-year-old girl? What exactly is it that makes people so untrusting and afraid of children? Just a couple of weeks ago the same woman kept following me around while I was shopping for clothes. She had followed me around so much that I had come to expect it and therefore ignore it. Yet, for some reason on a particular day my mind was boiling with thoughts of exasperation, injustice, and anger. "Why is she only following me? I can see so many other people here. Why me, why?" But I knew that these thoughts proved of no value. So I picked up two shirts off a rack and quickly turned toward her.

"Excuse me, but which one of these shirts do you think would look better on me?" I said authoritatively. I looked squarely into her green eyes while she blushed.

"Oh, um, I really do not know. I think they would both look fine."

I gazed down at the two shirts in my hands. I had been so intent on holding eye contact with her that I had not really looked at the shirts I had picked up. They were both the same style, but one was red, while the other was blue. Ideas started formulating in my head. I turned back to her, asking, "But which color do you prefer? Would the red one look better or the blue one? It's the same style shirt, just in different colors. I hope that you can help me."

Now she had turned extremely red. "I just cannot say; I think they both look nice," she replied quietly.

"Oh well, I guess I will buy them both." She looked into my deep brown eyes and said nothing. The next time that I went into that store she saw me and gave me an embarrassed smile. She has never followed me since that day.

My parents once said that there is nothing so gratifying as breaking a stereotype, and I have come to believe that this is true. I have never really realized how many people that I have changed in my life. I have changed the teachers who dared to assume that I would never excel in their classes because of the color of my skin. I have changed the minds of adults who thought that I would be rude and brash just because I am black. I have changed countless others, their names unknown, but I shall never forget their stunned expressions when I gave them an unwarranted smile, when I politely excused myself after accidentally bumping into them. I truly believe that all of the hatred in this world stems from fear, a fear of what we do not know. I think that we all need to gain the courage to overcome our fears. Only then can we actually know, appreciate, and love our fellow man, regardless of external appearance.

"*Okay, so who brought something for Martin Luther King Day? Nobody?*"

My teacher looked around at the twenty-some second-grade faces she saw and soon began to rest her gaze on me.

"*Iris? Not even you? You should have something if no one else. You should be so thankful to him that you should have been the first one to bring something.*"

I got scared. I had never been reprimanded like this, especially in front of the class. Up until that point I had not really seen my classmates and myself as that different from one another. And now my teacher was telling me how obviously different I was. Although I didn't understand it at the time, my teacher was, in fact, saying that it was my responsibility to teach the class, that because of my color and my rights I should somehow be thankful to all of them and teach them about Dr. Martin Luther King, Jr.

After her lecture I made some excuse about needing to use the bathroom and went out into the hall. I knew something was wrong, but I just couldn't identify what it was. I was sure that I should have known something about Martin Luther King, but I didn't know why I was the primary one who should have known.

Now I know exactly what was wrong and how I feel about it. It is disgusting that I was singled out in the class and made to feel like a lesser person than my classmates. What did come out of that experience is my ability to relate to others who have found themselves in a similar situation. That's why I was so amazed when I read Lynette's piece about an event so similar to mine.

THE TWENTY WORDS I NEVER UNDERSTOOD

Lynette Salik, 17

BLACK

I was in the second grade. I was seven or eight. I had no idea what the teacher meant. I thought it was odd, but I kept on coloring my picture. I don't remember what I was coloring exactly, but it was something I could bury my face in. It wasn't until years later that I began to understand. I think it happened in February, which made what she said kind of fitting.

Every day half of the class was in the reading circle and the other was at their desks. The teacher was sitting in the center of the circle and reading to the students, and I was at my desk half listening to what she was saying. I thought I heard something about slavery and black history. I tuned in to the last sentence, and it was as clear as a bell: "If it weren't for men like Martin Luther King, whites and blacks wouldn't be able to go to school together, huh, Lynette?"

I looked up puzzled, thinking, What did I do to earn such attention? I didn't know what she meant or why she had called my name. I just gave a confused nod, and went back to coloring. The only reason I remember it at all was because of the expression on her face when I looked up. It was an exaggerated wink and a half smile that looked like the smile of an ogress who had just eaten a small child. Now, looking back, I realize I was the only black girl in my class and one of two in my entire grade.

About seven years after that, I was doing community service at my elementary school and I ran into her. She remembered me. She remembered my name. I was surprised, honestly shocked; I didn't know how to feel. This woman had had an effect on me that shaped the way I walk into new social situations, and all I could do was stand there. I didn't see her again for the rest of the day, not that I would have known what to say if I saw her again. I can think of what I might say now, but in that exact moment I could barely breathe, let alone speak. I wanted to ask what she meant, I wanted to ask what gave her the right to say anything at all, but I realized that gave her too much power because I'd be hanging on her every word, waiting for her to resolve a major issue in my life and I need her to do that for me. All I could do was give a polite response. Then, she walked away. I looked around at all those little kids, Black, White, Asian, and all the colors of the rainbow, happily running around together, and wondered, Would they understand what I didn't? Would they just nod?

I can never escape from my identity. When I was younger I remember people telling me I did a great job or accomplished something wonderful. I remember thinking, Do they really think I did a good job or that a black girl did a good job? I have always been strongly connected with being a black girl, and although I am proud of it, it is not all that encompasses me. In school I am so often referred to as the black girl, or the dark one. I am not ashamed that they notice this, but in some cases I wonder how the people who identify me this way would feel if I only saw them as white and constantly said, "Oh the white girl over there," or "The white boy did that?" Sometimes I would like to be pointed out as, "Oh, that's the girl who is smart," not just "Oh, that's the black girl."

In her poem "You Are You But I Am Black," Jasmin portrays the feeling of being seen only as a person of color—but not really a person. Jasmin touched on something that has bothered me for a while, and with her words I was able to better understand my own feelings.

YOU ARE YOU BUT I AM BLACK

Jasmin Kolu Zazaboi, 12
LIBERIAN / EUROPEAN AMERICAN

The black man walked down the street
You are you but he is black.
The little black girl played hopscotch on the walk,
You are you but she is black.
Pretty cool for a black guy,
Less human or less respect?
How come you are you,
But I am black?

In *Toi Derricotte's powerful book* The Black Notebooks, *she examines internalized racism—the racist thoughts, opinions, and images that people of color have unconsciously internalized. In one part, Derricotte even writes of her own feelings about her husband's dark skin and her disgust with it.*

After reading this book and having a few conversations with friends, I felt very angry and also very relieved. I was relieved because I had read a book by a wonderful author that I could relate to and I could understand completely. As she talked of her own struggle with internalized racism, I thought of mine. I thought of how I have always thought, "the lighter the better"; and although I hate to admit it, I have always idolized white girls and disliked my own sisters of color. I recalled how I used to spend hours combing, brushing, blow-drying, straightening, and curling my own hair just to get the look that came so naturally to white girls.

As I've grown older I've learned to accept and appreciate who I am and become aware of my own internalized racism. I also know it is not my fault. As long as I see white as beautiful on television, movies, magazines, and in society, I will feel this way. In "A Page from My Diary: Black and Beautiful," Lianne shares with us how it feels to be dark-skinned. I would like to salute Lianne for her honesty, and I hope that soon we can all see people of color as beautiful and magnificent.

A PAGE FROM MY DIARY: BLACK AND BEAUTIFUL

Lianne Labossiere, 17
BLACK HAITIAN AMERICAN

I am not confident in who I am as a Black girl. To be utterly honest and blunt, I have trouble accepting Black as beautiful. I believe this is a feeling many dark-skinned girls like myself have.

I am talking about the hair and skin color stereotypes within the Black community, where the lighter you are the better, the curlier your hair is the better off you are. These are things that you learn as a little girl, and they follow you through your life. They follow you through middle school, when you sit for hours while your mother passes a hot iron through your hair to get it somewhat straight. Or when you apply lots of gel so that your "natural curls" will show. It is with you when you decide to get a perm. And it has always hurt me to hear people say (although I do admit to having said it myself, just to fit in), "I better get out of the sun because I really don't need to get any darker," as if getting darker is a bad thing.

I am born to a Caribbean family, and these views are just as strong if not stronger in the Caribbean than in the States. In the Caribbean, it's the whiter, the better, from skin tones to hair texture. The tones in my family run from a very pale to a very dark color. But for some reason, I have always felt very self-conscious because I am so dark. On my mother's side, two of my six aunts are dark-skinned and beautiful. Yet I have always seen them as exceptions to the rule. On my father's side, only two of the seven brothers married dark-skinned women. All the others, including my father, married women with light skin and long hair. This has always made me feel that being lovely and being "red" are synonyms.

In school, the feeling that lighter is better continued. Nobody wants to have "nappy" hair. I really felt that getting a perm would end my days of hair trouble; now I regret giving in to society's views on beauty. And I express my regret for those who are the darkest shade of ebony, because I know the teasing and tormenting they must endure. It is not easy being called "Back to Africa Black" by people only a few shades lighter than you. Beautiful today is not nappy hair or dark skin. And it's tough growing up and feeling that you will never be beautiful, no matter what. The media applies pressure, but families and friends can unconsciously make it more personal.

You mean to tell me that I have to get a perm to straighten my hair, buy blue contacts, and bleach my skin to be beautiful? That's a price I really can't afford to pay. Yet that is the message being fed to children all over this nation every day. I think that as Blacks we need to start looking for beauty within our own culture. We need to tell our dark-skinned ladies that they are beautiful. We need to seriously start loving our "nappy" hair and our ebony shades. Otherwise we are denying ourselves and missing out on all the beauty around us. Maybe, if when I was growing up, someone had told me I was beautiful, even if my hair wasn't curly or straight, even if my skin was dark, even if my nose was wide, perhaps I would not have such a problem today in believing Black truly is beautiful.

One of my first memories of blatant racism was when I went shopping with my new stepfather for a birthday cake for my mother. Mike is a big, tall Native American with long hair. Because of his size he looks menacing (especially to white people where we live, where Native Americans are systematically discriminated against), but underneath he is a kind, intelligent, and caring person. As we approached the bakery of our local grocery store, we were first in line. The white woman behind the counter looked us over with obvious disdain. Then she turned to the white couple next to us and asked if she could help them.

I glanced up at Mike and saw a little anger in his face, but he seemed to be primarily focusing his attention on finding the right cake. Unlike him, I was furious. I was in fifth grade, and until that point I'd had the silly notion that workers in stores were there to help me find what I wanted and to be nice about it. When eventually we left the store with the birthday cake, I was fuming. As we walked to the car I discussed how I felt with Mike, how the woman should be fired, and how from now on I would never shop at that store.

Mike listened. After I was finished expressing my contempt for the situation, he told me it was normal. He shared many examples of obvious racism just like the one we encountered and then said soon, as much as he hated to admit it and did not want it to happen, I would have a list of examples similar to his.

Mike was right. Now, at age seventeen, I can't even begin to count the number of times I have been helped last, treated poorly, or followed in stores. Just as Mike said it would, racism has become a part of my life; and as much as I hate the experience and become enraged every time I encounter it, it still exists. What is even worse is that there is almost no escaping it. I still shop in the same grocery store because it is the closest to me; I still walk on the same street because it is mine; and I still eat in the same restaurants because they are the only ones in my small city. I cannot help but participate in these systems because they are a part of my life, and although I may be treated badly, followed, or stared at, I cannot escape them.

In "Racism," Lisbeth speaks of her own experiences in restaurants, in stores, and in dealing with stereotypes. It saddens me to think that these experiences occur and to know they are not unique to Lisbeth and myself.

RACISM

Lisbeth Pelayo, 16
LATINA

As a Latina, I have experienced racism in my life. For example, in restaurants, cities, and in some shopping centers. I remember going to a nice restaurant; we came in before a white family, but they served them first and hardly paid attention to us when we called them. I've also been to some restaurants that have white cashiers and a Latino/a sweeping or cleaning. They pay the white people more and promote them more often that the Latino/a. When I go with my cousins to Beverly Hills to shop, the white people who are there shopping or working are always checking us out, like we're not supposed to be there.

You also get stereotypes, such as when I went to my cousin's house. Her friends were there, and they are white. When they saw me, they immediately started to ask me questions like what gang I was in. I said, "What? I'm not even in a gang." They said, "Oh, sorry." But they were still afraid of me because I told them I go to school in East L.A. I felt put down a little, but it didn't matter to me because I don't really care what a bunch of white girls think of me, as long as my family and I know it's not true. That's all that matters.

Having light skin has always affected how I am treated. When I attended an all-white school I was not seen as a shade of black, but instead as just black. When I attended a more diverse school, I was no longer just a black girl, but a light-skinned black girl. I noticed that instead of really knowing me, people assumed that I talked "proper," that I was liked more by guys, and that I could relate more to white people. I also realized that there was a wall set up between myself and my darker-skinned peers. As close as we were, we all realized that because of my light skin I was given certain privileges that they were not given.

I am still struggling with this reality, but in writing this book I have realized that I am not the only one. I received many pieces from girls who have to deal with the consequences of their light or dark skin. It's comforting to know that there are others who are experiencing the same conflict and are willing to share their stories.

Kazia's story wonderfully depicts what she goes through as a light-skinned black female. She lets us know of the heartaches she experiences, the way she deals with them, and her desire to be closer to all those of her race. I learned a lot from Kazia's words.

COMPLEXION

Kazia T. Steele, 17

BLACK

"Light-skinned people get everything." I hear this quote and many others like it all the time. I kind of understand why my dark-toned peers say these things. In our society it seems that if a person is close to the white skin tone, it automatically makes them beautiful and able to attain success easily. This belief caused me to get verbally degraded in school. I handled it the best way I could, but there is only so much a person can take. You can be the strongest person in the world mentally, but if a person had to endure the comments I had to put up with, they would at some point be broken down. I am a product of two dark-toned African Americans who just happened to be born light-skinned (genes tend to be funny that way). Of course, being born of a black family I am going to identify myself as a black person, but my peers thought otherwise. From primary to middle school I attended predominately white schools. So of course I would cling to whatever small number of blacks we had in school, not because I wanted to separate myself from white people but because I felt more comfortable around my own people.

Even though I was very social, I made sure to put my studies first. I have been blessed to receive the gift of acquiring and retaining knowledge with ease. My schools noticed this gift and put me in advanced classes. I was the only black student in these classes, and this situation separated me from my black friends. The only way I could associate with them was at lunch. My peers quickly turned on me and accused me of being "white" and "high yellow." This was a shock to me; these were supposed to be my friends, the ones I could go to for support. Where was I to turn now? I was in an all-white class. Yes, I had white friends in the class, but they always made sure to remind me that I was black. There was no way of fitting in to the white group. I was stuck. I knew I was black, and I couldn't understand why my black friends couldn't see it anymore.

I thought I knew who I was, but with all of this questioning, I found myself changing in order to fit in with my so-called friends again. I started to notice that I often degraded my complexion through humor to hide the hurt when the subject of black skin tones was being discussed. I found myself putting down any so-called race impurities found in my family's background. Even though I was called almost everything in the English vocabulary to describe my skin tone, I was never called Oreo. I would have accepted that better than Mello-Yello, because at least with being an Oreo you get some distinction of being black.

I also took on some physical actions to make myself appear more "black." I would stand outside in the sun for a couple of hours to make my skin darker. Of course this did not work. I was young at the time, and I just wanted to fit in. Now that I am seventeen years old and have learned about my background and where my family has come from, I am proud of my skin tone. On a regular basis I now find myself associating better with light-skinned people, not because I don't want to hang out with my dark-toned friends, but because I feel support and we have gone through the same things. Now I have accepted the fact that I am never going to get darker, and in my heart I know I am black. I just hope that my dark-toned peers accept that also.

Jasmin's poetry is beautiful. She sent me a package of six poems, and all of them had an incredibly strong message and a great voice. "The Color Line" was the one I enjoyed the most. I kept it on my dresser for a while, almost as a personal anthem. It's short, true, and elegant.

THE COLOR LINE

Jasmin Kolu Zazaboi, 12
LIBERIAN / EUROPEAN AMERICAN

I'm standing on the color line
I am black,
Yet I am white,
I am day,
But I am night,
I am an eclipse of beauty.

When I was in eleventh grade, I attended a conference in Tennessee on oppression. While I was there I met a girl who looked a lot like me, with light skin and curly hair. As we talked I asked her what race she was, and she replied that she was multiracial. She then went on to tell me about her Cuban father and his parents and then her biracial mother and her mother's black and white parents. All the while I sat in amusement, wondering how she must feel about all of this. I know personally that being biracial has caused me to question my own identity and my place in society. When I asked her how she felt about this, she looked at me, surprised. She said, "What do you mean how do I feel? This is how I am and I am beautiful this way." She then went on to explain how she is incredibly proud of herself and if she were any other way, as she put it, she would be bored with herself.

After our conversation I began to really understand what she was saying. Instead of searching for a way to fit in to society, I can accept who I am and expect society to find a place for me. Instead of identifying with one race, I can be proud of all of my ancestors and speak of all of them.

In this book's second poem called "The Color Line," this one by Jade

Pagkas-Bather, the realities of being biracial are explored. Being biracial is and can be difficult, but it's always a little better when you know that people like Jade are out there experiencing the same thing and writing about it with such passion.

THE COLOR LINE

Jade Pagkas-Bather, 17
JAMAICAN/GREEK

"It looks like we're going backwards because we're facing
   backwards"
She said
"Oh," I muttered in an imaginary voice
"I understand," again. In a voice that did not exist
If only everything were so simple
A-ha!
And everything like that
Little lost girl on the red line blues
Where all I see are Black faces
And liquor stores—good news
Lonely White girl sits alone
I sympathize with her
Partly because she's the only White girl
And partly because I know what it's like to be
The lightest person on this train
"Good luck trying the 'I'm an Albino' line"
"Really?"
"Yeah—good luck"
I think I'm here because I know
Exactly what I want
I want to not have a headache
And not have to worry about numbers

And letters and STUFF
Black face
Black hair
Black neighborhood
'Cept for the Mexicano dozing off
I sit in the middle of the train car
Significance?—maybe
Just another Black/White baby
I'm riding the color line
Because it amuses me
Because Black people understand
Me the best way they know how
Because White people abuse me
In their quest to remain P.C.
47th-lady with AFRO exits the color line
I miss her and I don't even know her
Her face was friendly
And she seemed like she'd pat me on the head
And say, "yes, little 'latto. I understand"
But, she wouldn't
At least the sun is shining now
And that annoying man with the oils
Isn't still trying to get me to say "Hello" to him
And that White man
Who sat next to me 'cause I looked "safe enough"
Isn't still trying to blend into my skin
Chinatown—I guess Yellow is right
Between Black and White
If I go home
Will that be my way of peeling off my colors?
Is it because I know Mommy
Will still love me no matter what my shade or hue will be?
All I know is I'm riding the color line

And my colors are sitting next to me
In the middle of the car
Fighting their own war
The war that has been fought
Forever in my veins
Maybe I am riding the color line
Because I know nothing
And nothing knows me
Or maybe I'm trying to find myself
Or lose myself
I'm cold
And the tunnels are dark
And White people are entering the car
I don't feel so sorry for Girl X anymore
The Black folks
Are empty, trying to burn the faces
Of the White folks
With ignorance and blank looks
Nonchalance
But, I'm here in the middle
I've always been here
And I'm not getting off the color line
Because the music at the
Jackson stop reminds me
That I'm not some little lost girl
I come from a people with steel drums
And brave political leaders
I come from a people with
Brains and culture
Olives and mangos
And mathematics and Blue Mountains
Within my veins
There is no distinction

As I grow older
I realize why the Black folks pretend
Not to see the White folks
It is because the Black folks
Are afraid of looking at themselves

In this piece, Faleesha writes of how hard it is to be multiracial and harassed because of it. When one does not have a specific race to identify with, a racial slur can hurt even more because of that lack of identification and belonging.

IT'S HARD

Faleesha Grady, 14
BLACK/WHITE

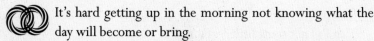 It's hard getting up in the morning not knowing what the day will become or bring.

It's hard walking down the dark halls as I take deep breaths; I tell myself ignore, just ignore. As some kids yell racial slurs; blacks call me Oreo and whites call me Nigger. The Hispanics call me a traitor, but am I a traitor?

Why don't they understand you CAN be mixed with black and white? You CAN have regular black and white friends.

It's not my fault the Hispanics think I'm Hispanic; it's not my fault the whites think I'm only white; it's not my fault that the blacks think I'm only black; it's not my fault I am the way I am.

I don't have to have blond hair and blue eyes to be white. I don't have to have a dark chocolate complexion to be black either, and I CAN be both.

They just don't understand. It's hard being a mixed black and white teen. It's hard walking down the hall getting called names. It's hard not knowing who I should trust.

One of the lessons I think all girls of color learn is tolerance. We are taught to be tolerant of our families, our friends, and our society. We are rarely seen as outspoken, and when we are it is almost always because we are defending others. Tolerance to me is what has also kept us all quiet for so long about sexism. We have been told that we as females of color are betraying men of color when we stand up for women's rights.

This is not true. When we fight against derogatory name calling, catcalls, and other ways in which we are oppressed as women, we are telling all men that we will not accept their behavior. We are standing up for all women, and by doing so we are enabling ourselves to be less tolerant of bad behavior and more active. We need to learn that catcalls, sexist jokes, inappropriate touching, and disrespect to our bodies and ourselves are just as offensive as racist jokes, derogatory comments, and abuse based on race. Sexism is running rampant, just as racism is, and it is important that we as girls of color refuse to tolerate it.

In "Searching for a Little Respect," *Elsie reminds us of the mistreatment we endure. Thank you, Elsie, for sharing this with us, speaking out and not being tolerant.*

SEARCHING FOR A LITTLE RESPECT

Elsie M. Giron, 17

HISPANIC

Ladies, I know you can relate to this: "Hey girl, come here, let me get them digits!" or "Damn girl, let me tap that ass!"

Some boys think that kind of behavior is appealing and that we are actually attracted to that nonsense. They are wrong. I know for a fact that I'm not the only one who gets offended when these words are called out. I'm tired of putting up with the ignorance of these boys. I've noticed that when boys come up to me, the first things that pop from their mouths are sexist comments. All they care to see is what I'm wearing. They don't see anything past that. They don't care about how many AP classes I take or how many languages I speak.

I want some respect.

At least some of them are honest. Others pretend to be interested and turn out to be the biggest hypocrites we've ever encountered. Like a boy I was getting to know. We had PE together, and one day he approached me. He was incredibly sweet and polite. We had great conversations in class, and eventually he asked for my phone number. I don't usually give out my number, but I had a crush on him. He was funny and charming, gave me lots of advice regarding my schoolwork, and applauded me when I did well. To make a long story short, he turned out to be a jerk. He lied and told all of his friends that he slept with me. When I asked him about it, he denied that whole thing. He broke my heart.

I know what else you can relate to, ladies. I know we all like guys to be nice and smooth when they are trying to get with us. We like guys who come up with a decent line instead of those played-out lines. Or a guy who could do the old-fashioned thing, who can just walk away without saying the "B" word. All we need is a little respect. Right, ladies? Is that too much to ask? I think not.

When I was younger my mother used to subscribe to Essence *magazine for me. I would sit in my room going over all the pages, mesmerized by all the beautiful black faces. I knew my mother purchased the magazine for me not because of the articles but because it actually had people my color in its pages. However, as much as I loved the magazine, I always wished my mother would have instead purchased* Glamour *or* YM. *I wanted to see all the pretty white young faces telling me I, too, could be one of them. I wanted to know the fashion for young people, advice about boys, and most of all beauty tips to help me look "prettier."*

I now try not to read those magazines because the result is destructive. I was never able to successfully lighten my cheeks or get the perfect guy, and the magazines just ended up making me feel inadequate. Still a little part of me wondered—like Cecilia wonders in her poem "All-American Girl"—what it would be like if I were white?

ALL-AMERICAN GIRL

Cecilia Nguyen, 15
VIETNAMESE

Hands glide over the slick magazine ad
Filled with now white skin,
Sun-kissed strands fixed to perfection,
And long, toned legs.

It would be strange being one of them—
One of the girls in the magazine,
A white girl.

I would have a chance of being tall
And of having creamy, acne-free skin.
Just another face in the crowd
Instead of one of two minorities in a class.
Wouldn't feel awkward when talk points to 'Nam.

But never

To celebrate Chinese New Year,
To have Asian Pride with every new Jackie Chan movie,
To be stereotyped as a "computer nerd,"
To have my parents,
To be me.
Wouldn't it be strange if I were white?

I didn't start shaving my legs until I was in sixth grade. I didn't want to, but I did it because one of the white popular girls at my school told me to. She said my legs were hairy and if I wanted to get any guys I would need to shave them.

I did as she said and soon hoped to get guys, whatever that meant. It didn't work, and instead I was forced to continue shaving my legs because of the pressure of everyone around me. I wanted to be accepted and in order to be I thought I would need to do things "their" way. After I started shaving my legs I began to dress like the popular white girls. Then I styled my hair like them, acted like them, and slowly tried to become them. It was not that I really liked them or wanted to be them but rather that I wanted to be accepted by them.

Up until that point I had never felt fully accepted and strongly wanted that feeling.

As I grew older I realized I really did not want to be like them. I began to style my hair the way I wanted to and dress the way I felt comfortable. I began, I think, to be me.

In her piece "Chameleon," Anne speaks of how she has always wanted to be appreciated and understood. She is a biracial female, who, like myself, has felt the pain of not being accepted and of putting on a false front to please others.

CHAMELEON

Anne Hoye, 18
AFRICAN AMERICAN

As an eighteen-year-old girl preparing to embark upon a journey into a world of challenging new experiences, I am struggling with being both adopted and biracial. Throughout my life, my greatest difficulties and hardships have resulted from my need to be accepted. As I look ahead, I am compelled to reflect back upon the experiences which have touched my life. In the words of an ancient Chinese proverb, "Life is like a piece of paper on which every passerby leaves a mark." Various people and experiences in my life have touched me in a way that has left me with a sense of fear, not a fear of life or of those experiences waiting for me, but a fear of being alone.

The theme of my life has become isolation. I am so afraid to love now because every time I allow myself to become attached to someone, I end up having to fend for myself when they leave me. My heart has been painfully ripped apart, piece by piece, and I have been left with nothing. As a direct result of this, my ability to maintain, or even to begin a deep relationship with another person has been weakened by those who continue to walk in and out of my life.

I believe that the root of much of my anguish began with my adoption at birth. Even though I have been raised in a loving home my entire life, a small part of me can't help but feel unwanted. This feeling of isolation got off to a running start when I was a young girl, with the anger and bitterness I felt toward the woman who gave birth to me and was able to just shut me out of her life. Oftentimes I wondered if I just wasn't pretty enough, or smart enough, or even good enough to be called her own. Even though I still have these questions, as I have grown older I have also gained a better sense of understanding and acceptance.

All in an effort to be loved and accepted, I have spent my entire life concealing the real me beneath layers and layers of disingenuous laughter and smiles. I have taught myself to internalize everything and to conceal my emotions beneath a mask. I wear a mask that is beautiful and capable of being loved because my real face, which is ugly, covered in scars, and filled deeply with pain, seems to be the reason for my continuous sense of abandonment.

As a biracial child in today's society, I learned to relinquish my need to be accepted at a very young age. Even though this was at a time when my family placed little importance upon color, society did, so not being part of one large, identifiable group caused a great sense of confusion in my life. As a remedy, I would go around believing and preaching to others that I wasn't black but "cocoa," as my mother called me. This innocent idea became my form of identity and gave me a place to *belong*. I was attached to this idea until my older sister warned me that people were not going to see me as "cocoa," but rather as black. She advised me to accept reality. At that moment, I began to realize that I needed to confront the issues relating to my color.

I established a mind-set in which I simply considered myself to be black because everyone I have been associated with saw me as just that. My "identity" has always been made up of what others see me as, not as I see myself. I thought by calling myself black, I was making things easier. Instead, I've complicated matters. I now face the black community who resents the way I walk, talk, and act. Because of my mixed heritage, they call me anything but black, denying me the right to identify myself the way I want. To them I am mixed, mulatto, or just a "shy little white girl." When I attempt to identify myself with the white community, they see my tinted skin color and take into account the "one drop rule," in which one drop of black blood makes you black. Apparently, I am too black to be white and too white to be black. There is no middle ground.

I've struggled my whole life to be many different things for many different people. Somehow, I've become a chameleon, always able to appear as something I am not. Despite my deep desire for people to come to really know me, I've become accustomed to living under a false persona, convincing myself that the real me has nothing worth being loved. Although being a chameleon may appear to have its advantages, it has failed to allow the real me to shine through. I've decided that during the next phase of my journey, I will inaugurate a brand-new way of expressing myself: *truthfully*.

Tara's pieces were some of the first that I received (her other piece appears later in this section). I needed them not only for the book but for myself. I needed to be reminded of how important this book was and that all the struggles I went through to make it happen were worth it. Her words convey an awesome anger that I think many of us are familiar with.

This is one piece that I feel all girls of color can relate to. I cannot recall all the many times I have felt alone, angry, uncomfortable, fake, unwanted, ignored, and disgusted, all within the walls of my school. Tara's poem describes this feeling, within the framework of a field hockey game, and I thank her so much for sharing her writing with us.

UNTITLED

Tara Bynum, 19
AFRICAN AMERICAN

Half time.

Ten girls scramble onto the green brilliance of the field, dressed in red scattered throughout their thick blue uniform

Hair and face

Ready to lift their voices in chant and cheer . . .

Our team is what RED HOT . . . Our team with an educational mission to provide young girls with a positive education that will lift their self-esteem and make them ready to become leaders for the future of America.

Our team is what RED HOT . . . Our team. A little less than ten years ago I said yes to the beige envelope that sat waiting for me on my mother's bed. Ten years ago I became a part of that RED HOT team . . . ten years ago I signed my life away only to be reborn a better person.

Our team is RED HOT, R-E-D, red H-O-T hot, you can't be the stuff that we got

Racism. Classism.

Droning in the back of my mind the sounds of onlookers at this field hockey game dancing comically to the tune of offbeat chanters while their blond and mousy brown ponytails blow in the breeze as they watch classmates slamming their feet into the soft sod banging the small white ball against their brown wooden sticks hoping again for that championship flag to hang proudly among others in our gym.

A SCREAM thundering against the dull brown barks of the trees and the light brown bricks of the building.

One point for us. Yeah, the amusement of such events always passes me by, even though I am always slightly entertained by the girls dancing around in their bright red uniforms with their faces painted various hues of red.

Young girls ready for the fight of war fought with a ball and a gently curved stick the fight for conformity, homogeneity. A lost fight because there I am a spot of darkness, a Negro,

—Oh the term is no longer used

—A colored

—Still fifty years behind

—The black . . .

Girl waiting patiently with other young Negro children to leave the discomforts of the limestone bricks, the gaze of uncomfortable parents eager to remove their children from the dark presence that is beginning to engulf

School. A child runs past waving a field hockey stick haphazardly in her arms, screaming out the names of friends that scream R-E-D red, H-O-T hot

Friends

Who all seem to run together into one mundane pool, SuziJenLizBethLaurenSusieJenBethLaurenLiz,

Of white girls with nameless faces representing the grandness of high society.

We joke amongst ourselves, finding simple amusement in the subtle bigotries of our beloved school

—Yeah, she calls her dog Tarbaby, we should get a white dog and call it Cracker . . .

—Hey Monica, I'm Sabrina, Okay Monica, I'm Sabrina, Monica will you come here please,

I AM SABRINA

Or rather just another face running into the next, searching for recognition, an identity somewhat separate from the color of my skin, caught

Unable to break myself free from the confines of the linoleum-covered floors the uniform skirts and questions surrounding the upkeep of my nappy hair. Yet, somehow enjoying every minute every second of constantly trying to retain an identity while slowly being swept head-on into the lives of others simply because of the brown undertones of my skin.

—Okay, let's discuss the civil rights movement

my body cringes and my heart skips a beat, the teacher's head slowly turns in my direction, the sun pressed against the whiteness of her skin, her wrinkles softly protruding from her concealer and flesh makeup, and into my eyes she stares, her baby blue wells of ignorance prepared with the rest of face to ask,

—Okay Monica, could you tell us a little bit about it . . . my face is red and my ears burn

—My name is, oh never mind. May I be excused

My legs begin to move from around the desk and I leave to get a drink of water or some form of relief, eight months in that class and she still does not know my name, not to mention I have not read the civil rights chapter nor did I live through it three months ago it was slavery, hopefully we won't make it to welfare reform . . . thinking as the wetness of the water glides down my throat.

I breathe

And enter the room again as the woman before me rambles on about the excellence of JFK and his civil rights legislation referencing back to the war of 1865 and how Lincoln fought for the freedom of

The Slave . . .

We joke, what's up Monica, What's up Monica. Oh my fault my name is Monica, not like they can tell us apart anyway. The laughter is enormous, belting across the white linoleum, other tables stare but slowly for only an hour our darkness is forgotten, the racism is forgotten the classism is forgotten. We become children like all others shucking and jiving, discussing adolescent life and the youthful middle eastern that has

Caught my

Eyes

A teacher walks out of the teacher's lounge a smile crosses her lips, we simply gaze no friendship exists between us to her we are a threat that they pay her to teach

—What time does your bus leave . . . . the hands of the clock slowly reach to the eight and the momentary sanity is shattered as I enter the hallway prepared to brave the next in a line of classes

Another SCREAM . . . two more points for us and the ambiguous mob cheers loudly as our competitors slump their heads in growing misery. We are closer than ever to winning yet another championship game, another flag to hang from the scaffolding in our gym.

Suddenly everyone, including me, becomes engulfed in a monstrous wave of school spirit, the shouts spread through our lungs, the chants begin.

Be Aggressive . . . Be Aggressive . . . B-E-A-GG-R-E-SS-I-V-E . . .

I have been told numerous times that I am too angry—that my anger is misguided or that it's a personal thing and I shouldn't take it out on others— that when someone is oppressed I should relax and not worry.

I have yet to understand what "too angry" means. I don't understand why it is that when I am called a bitch, a ho, a nigger, or an oreo, I shouldn't retaliate. I don't understand why it is that when I express myself, I am "too angry," but when my white guy friend does, he is justified. I'm an assertive young woman of color who is sick, tired, and, yes, angry, and fully justified in that anger.

In "Sick and Tired," Andrea captures one of the ways anger affects me—to make me sick and tired of oppression.

SICK AND TIRED

Andrea Friaz-Gallardo, 17
MEXICAN AMERICAN / CHICANA

I am sick and tired
Of
White people being
Sick and tired.

I am sick and tired
Of always—
Having to teach them,
Defend myself
I am sick
And tired
Of being the
One.

Sick and tired of doubting myself
Blamed, attacked
Sick and tired
Of being
Sick and tired
And hearing themmmmmmm

Be si   ck
And
Ti   red.

Sickandtired—
Of   what?
Being privileged?
Spoon-fed? Handed Success?
Being   what?
Doingwhat?
Being   white?

Try being brown.

"*Assimilation*" is another piece by Andrea, which also touches on important issues. The process of assimilation is something we've become so accustomed to and comfortable with that we no longer know when we are taking part in it. Many Americans have lost their own languages, cultures, and heritages, and we are instead drifting into a homogenous American society based on materialism—a society that has no real culture.

My parents discuss assimilation because my stepfather, who is Native American, works hard to keep his language, culture, and traditions alive. I've heard them talk about the fact that many people mistake assimilation for diversity. The truth is that they're not the same thing at all. True diversity honors and accepts all languages, cultures, and traditions, whereas assimilation crushes them.

Andrea makes note of all that is lost in the assimilation process. The poem's repetition of the word "language" is haunting and memorable.

ASSIMILATION

Andrea Friaz-Gallardo, 17
MEXICAN AMERICAN/CHICANA

The first thing to go when you arrive is language.
In order to survive you must learn the dominant language.

No matter how you speak it, they will not accept you,
Because if it isn't your first, you can never speak the language.

Once you forget your own, it will never be yours again
And you are stuck with their language.

Your people will look at you in scorn for forgetting.
And you will weep and explain yourself in words not in your
    language.

A part of you will be lost, and you will look for it with all your might,
In libraries with books written in the wrong language.

Your name will be butchered into a million unrecognizable pieces,
Andree-ah they will say in a pronunciation foreign to your language.

Andrea you will protest and repeat again and again,
But it will never be said correctly in their language.

You'll lose your voice protesting and correcting
You will be weakened and be lost to their language

The heartbeat of your language will continue within you,
But you will be deaf to anything but their language.

*M*oving me to another school in second grade was my mom's idea. And on the first day of school I wasn't sure how good the idea was. I was surrounded by tons of kids who already knew one another and was forced to sit with the three other new kids.

After welcoming us and showing us to our desks, my teacher had the class sit in a circle. She then proceeded to fill out a sheet of paper, reporting statistics about our class. She muttered each one to herself and then filled in the appropriate answer. It started with boy-to-girl ratio, and then range of ages. Then she muttered to herself about black students in the class. I heard her say, "Two," and I immediately looked around. I saw one black girl and then knew the other one must be me.

I sat there angry and confused. The problem wasn't that the teacher was collecting that information, but instead how she had done it. I knew that I was black, but that I was other things, too. I wanted my teacher to see all the sides of me, not just the black side.

Later I realized that it was not that I was ashamed of that side, but I felt that I was showing shame for my other sides if they were not noticed. Now I want to show off all of my sides, the Jewish side, the West Indian side, and the European side. I feel that when I am taking a standardized test, or when I am asked my race, I am torn between either acknowledging all of my ancestors or just stating what everyone already thinks I am: black.

Alicia's problem is similar to mine. We cannot define ourselves using one term and find it hard to fit into the available options for identity. Alicia is comfortable with the term "Other"; however, I feel I have yet to feel it. Identity is a tough issue and when one is known as "Other," defining one's self can make it even harder. I admire Alicia's comfort with herself and hope that some-day I too can learn to define myself the way I want to and not care when I am labeled as "Other."

KNOWN AS "OTHER"

Alicia Mazzara, 17
CHINESE/ITALIN

On a Saturday in the not-so-distant past, I found myself filling out the microscopic bubbles on the name and address sections of my SAT score sheet. As on virtually all standardized tests I've ever taken, there is a box where it requests that you enter your race. "Please indicate your ethnic background." This is a simple enough question, isn't it? Well, not exactly. I stare at the various choices, already knowing which bubble I am condemned to darken: the one labeled "Other."

My father is Italian and my mother is Chinese, but there's no bubble that says "Italian/Chinese" on it. There is a bubble labeled Asian and a bubble labeled White, both of which apply to me. Yet I can't simply pick one, because I'm not exclusively White, nor am I exclusively Asian. Standardized tests are just another reminder that, try as I might to find a label fitting of my identity, the majority of people in America are of Caucasian descent.

Teenagers spend a lot of time trying to figure out how to "fit in." Fit in. What does that even *mean*? And why is it so important to so many? And what if you don't fit in? Is that so wrong? Because it's going to be some time in coming before "Multiracial" is part of the status quo. I don't want to play into a stereotype, but it's hard to deny that most young people are at least somewhat appearance- and image-conscious. Clothing, hairstyle, cliques—it all comes from somewhere. There are the conflicting urges to follow the norms of the social scene you are (or want to be) a part of, and yet still work to strike out a unique identity for yourself. And amidst all this, I've come to conclude that I am not part of the status quo and maybe, just maybe, that's okay.

The most glaring proof of this is that I'm not a member of the white majority. Yet it's actually not that glaring a point. I look somewhat

Italian. And I look somewhat Chinese. But I don't have the stereotypical earmarks, such as almond-shaped eyes, or a wide, flat nose. My
skin has a slight yellowish cast to it—essentially it's white in color.
Ironically, people who don't know me usually think I'm Jewish. I
guess the bottom line is that people can't seem to correctly figure out
what I am, white or yellow. Sometimes I feel like a sort of impostor,
calling myself a minority or person of color, when I feel like most
people couldn't tell the difference at first glance. For the most part,
the only difficulty my ethnic background has caused is a sort of internal identity crisis. Though I've witnessed plenty of ignorance about
Chinese culture, the only incident of racism I remember was in pre-
school when a little boy made a crack about me doing laundry. I
didn't have the faintest idea what he was talking about. Not until several years later did I learn what "chink" meant and why the Chinese
are insultingly referred to as laundrymen.

Though my face might betray it, I live with each foot firmly
planted in two different worlds which swirl together to form a
unique experience I can only call my own. Food and family are highly
prized in both Italian and Chinese cultures. As a result, I love to eat (I
know that makes me sound like a little piglet, but it's true), and I've
had the pleasure/pain of sampling many types of unusual fare. No-
table examples include shark's fin, tripe, and chicken knees. (I don't
recommend the chicken knees.) Also, I'm very close with my
extended family. My mother is from a family of six, and large family
dinners are frequent occurrences. I see and have seen my grandma
on a near-daily basis since I was a baby. The first words out of my
mouth were Cantonese, and though I can't speak much anymore, the
familiar guttural sounds and some of their meanings have been per-
manently seared into my memory bank. I am dismayed that for many,
being this close to one's extended family is nothing more than a
memory of a bygone era. Yes, there are drawbacks to having lots of
nosy Chinese relatives who like to ask personal questions of you at
the public dinner table, but for all the teasing, a part of me is desper-
ately clinging to everything they stand for. People die. Kids grow up.

Everything changes. You can never recapture the moments just as you lived them; each is unique and precious unto itself.

It's extremely easy to make snap judgments about people based on a first impression. Certainly, none of us are innocent of the crime. And as alienated and contentious as I sometimes feel going to a small, private school where a vast majority of the faces are white, there is a nagging voice in the back of my mind that insists that no matter how much someone irritates me, there's more to them than the first impression. There is more to me than meets the eye, and I can't accurately be summed up into some bland label. Like taking standardized tests, labels are unavoidable, but they must be taken with a good-sized grain of salt, because they don't tell the whole story.

My background also lends me a heightened sensitivity to racial stereotypes. Frankly, I am extremely annoyed when people make these high-pitched donkey noises (for example, "ching chaw chee") when pretending to "speak" Chinese. Do people honestly think that's what the language sounds like? And do the ignorant noisemakers have any idea how utterly *absurd* they look and sound? Oftentimes I think I witness stupid, ignorant acts such as this because people don't realize I'm Chinese and find such ignorance not only insulting, but very irritating. As much as ignorance over Chinese culture irks me, I also realize that I would never want to be so ignorant about someone else's culture. We may have an obsession with political correctness in the country, but I'd rather keep my mouth shut and refrain from making judgments when I don't know about someone else's lifestyle and customs.

Consequently, this perspective has helped build the social circle I find myself in today. I'm proud to say that my closest friends are all from different ethnic backgrounds, as well as of completely divergent personality types. It is this multifaceted quality of the group that makes the friendships so rich, while also generating the most conflict among us. But it is perhaps from these disagreements that I see how important it is to try to understand what it's like in someone else's shoes. One's ethnic background and culture shape one's values and, consequently, the window with which they view the world. As fraught as my friendships are with learning, I am also painfully aware that I'm not part of the "majority" at school, and that's often a very hard and lonely road to walk down. Our eccentricities are what make us who we are, and often the pressure to play those down in order to fit into a certain social group is very strong.

Earlier this year, I was at a large family dinner when my uncle asked me what I considered myself as—Italian or Chinese. Before I could get the words out of my mouth, my mother replied, with a touch of scorn in her voice, "She's *American.*" She was trying to protect me from a potentially awkward and embarrassing situation, but I didn't mind fielding the question. I am an American. But I am also Chinese, just as much as I am also Italian. I am a girl, I am a writer, I am a poet, I am an artist. I'm Alicia, and there's no one label that is going to capture my identity. But if you want me to fill in the little bubbles on an SAT score sheet, I'll gladly check "Other." It may seem nebulous, but on the other hand, that leaves me plenty of room to define it any way I like.

I used to tell my mother that I had the best of friends. Not because they were actually good friends but because they were friends with me. My mother would tell me not to think this way and that they were the ones that were lucky to be friends with me. I listened, but never really believed her. I was positive I had picked the perfect group of people to be friends with because they actually liked me, a black girl. As I've grown older I still appreciate my friends and know that they are lucky to be friends with me, just as I am lucky to be friends with them.

Akemie's poem took me back to my younger days. I remember how much I wanted everyone to see me not just as a color but as a real person. Now I want people to see all of me, including my color. I am proud of my skin and my personality. Akemie's poem reflects a feeling I think many of us have encountered, wanting to be loved despite how we may appear or be. What I think we must do is to stop focusing on how others feel about us, and work to feel good about ourselves.

I Wish . . . I Wish . . . I Wish!!!

Akemie Cousin, 13
AFRICAN AMERICAN

I wish that they could see me,
For who I am.
I wish that they could love me,
For my insides.
Just because I am black,
I have to be treated differently.
Does my blood not flow like the white man next to me?
Does my soul not wish to be loved like any other person?
Just because I don't look the way you want me to,
You feel like you can brush me off.
I wish you could see the person behind this flesh
I wish . . . I wish . . . .
I wish you could see that you're not that much different from me.

Every day I wake at 6:30, get dressed, and head to school. As I get there I am looked at, not greeted, by all the white faces. I go to my locker and head straight to my first class. I no longer stand and socialize because the looks I receive are too much. As I attend my classes, I sit at the back of the room where I intend to remain quietly as I listen to the lesson of the day.

My big mouth does not always allow this to happen, however, and sometimes as I argue with the teacher or other students, I force myself to leave the room for fear of showing them my true emotions. As the day ends I try to leave as quickly as possible. Returning to the comfort of my own home with my own friends or family puts a small Band-Aid on the wound that was the day. As I go to bed and drift off into slumber, a few hours later I am awakened and the Band-Aid is quickly ripped off my fragile skin.

"Outbreak," by Tara Bynum, depicts my day, my life, and my feelings in a way that is astonishing. Thanks, Tara, for helping me understand my own feelings and realize that others think the same way.

OUTBREAK

Tara Bynum, 19
AFRICAN AMERICAN

Walking through the dull
Quiet atmosphere
Moving to the continuous beat
Of my sullen heart
Awaiting my inevitable fate
To once again enter the bustling white halls
To force myself
Into a world
So tight, congested and bitter

Where my smile
Is nothing more than a representation
Of my inner hatred
For the people
That secretly mock me
As I walk through the halls
Embittered
Alone
Silently wondering
Why?Why?Why?
Why have I forced myself
Into this sadness
Where my voice is nothing
More than an empty echo
Bouncing through tears
Of these ignorant children
Whose eyes have been covered
With learned racism and green money
That controls their every thought, whisper
Among many.
Who will never completely understand
Who I am or where I come from
Among more
Who will never know me
Or hear my real voice
That asks every day to be heard
Anger
That penetrates through every
Live and dead nerve in my frigid body
Ready to explode
Shading their faces with a residue
That they will never forget
As they try in vain to
Understand

The reason for my outburst
As I scream a thousand shrieking cries
For help that never seems to come
Forced
Bound
By hands and feet
To listen to their crazy antics
And anecdotes
Upset because they have to see my
Dark face every day
Embittered
Hatred
A sudden burst that courses
Through my heated living veins
Ready to explode
With the force and power to kill
Unwilling to accept this new reality
That I have been denied so long

OUR ROOTS

In many pieces of writing I received, girls expressed a strong sense of family, culture, and heritage. Some girls wrote about how they felt as daughters, sisters, or cousins, and some wrote about their family history. Many wrote about strong cultural traditions and others about the loss or transformation of culture.

This section includes our history, and where we are today. For young women of color it may be even more important for us to recognize and celebrate our roots. Without knowing and remembering the people and the places we come from, we lose one of the parts of us that make us especially strong.

Our Roots helps us find ties to the earth, our families, ourselves, and, most of all, each other.

My family is without a doubt the most important thing to me. I have always been raised to put family first and to know that they will be there for me when no one else is.

When my mother first married my stepdad, we would take numerous trips out to the Pine Ridge Reservation in South Dakota to visit his family. When we got there, we could always expect to see at least three or so of his seven siblings, plus cousins and whoever else decided to stop by. Before this I had been raised by my mother and had never experienced a "big family" atmosphere. At the house my stepgrandmother would cook up a storm: fry bread, Indian tacos, bean soup, and kabubu bread (skillet bread). These family feasts would serve one purpose and that would be to unite everyone.

My stepdad cherishes the time he was able to spend with his family. To this day he travels out there with my little brother, sister, and mother. However, I no longer go. Although I deeply love my extended stepfamily, I have begun to nourish other sides of my own culture and family heritage. While I have yet to find an extended family that I truly connect to, I am incredibly grateful for what I have. I just hope that someday I will be able to feel as close to a group of people as my stepdad and siblings feel toward their family.

In Andrea's piece she expresses that closeness with her family. In "The San Joaquin Valley," she makes us feel as though we are there with her and her family as they cherish the time they spend together. I am not only envious of her family, but incredibly thankful for my own.

THE SAN JOAQUIN VALLEY

Andrea Friaz-Gallardo, 17
MEXICAN AMERICAN/CHICANA

The beauty of California does not lie in its crowded cities, but in its fertile valleys. People usually only pass by this beauty on their way to somewhere bigger. They pass the long expanses of flat, yellowed grass and dry, gritty dirt, the fields and fields of agriculture and see nothing. Brown people live in Califas, California, that is. In this immense state lives my family. The San Joaquin Valley is lush with people, my people, and culture.

I pack my bags thinking—oh geez! "Mami, what's the weather like over there right now?" She'll reply, but I'll still not know what to pack. So I get no sleep that night, I'll have to stay up packing and in the end just throw anything in my bag. My family makes this trek two times a year, in the summer and at Christmas, to visit all of our relatives. My mom is the only one in her family to have ventured out of this valley. We go to a tiny town called Toniville, a few miles from

Porterville. Although I know people have never heard of it, I tell
them anyway.

Before I know it I'll be on an airplane flying from Seattle over
Mount Rainer and Mount Shasta and Oregon and finally arrive at
Fresno Airport. I can't wait to see all my little cousins, my *tios* and
tias. My sister and I always complain about how we're going to be
bored there and how we hate to baby-sit our little cousins, but that's
just pretend. They're all so cute.

I walk off the steep stairs of the plane into the open air, muggy
heat, and sun, which we've missed in Seattle. Luscious pine and fir
trees do not grow here. All is flat. My sister and I follow behind my
mom and dad, lugging our suitcases to the pick-up area. My *tio* Maike
waits outside in his Suburban. He'll say, "God, you guys are pale!" It
feels so good to see him. He has these great rosy cheeks with deep
dimples that make him seem to always be smiling. We make sport of
counting every brown person we see.

I lapse into quiet as we begin the long, hot, two-hour drive to
Toniville, where Mama Maria lives. All the windows are tinted and
the air-conditioning is on full blast. Anything less and we would all
cook in the 110-degree weather. I don't read or talk. I hear my parents in front catching up with my uncle. I stare out the window, mesmerized by the rows of oranges, olives, and other fruits.

California should be the capital of oranges. Forget Florida, they
don't even compete. Navel, Blood, Satsumas, Valencias. Oranges
sliced, peeled, and au naturel. With salt and chili. Then there is
fresh-squeezed orange juice or you can poke a hole in it and suck the
juice out. A fresh orange picked straight from the tree is best. Peeling
it, you get white powder all over your hands; then we'll crack the
window to let some of the acidy scent drift away.

The orange trees grow low to the ground, green thick oval leaves
branch out on all sides of the tree. On empty roads if you're hungry
and need a snack, you just stop and pick some. Be careful though,
if growers catch you they'll get mad. The sprinklers go on automatically and water the oranges. Finally when the oranges are ripe,

grossly underpaid Mexican farmworkers will subject themselves to pesticides, and the heat. They will climb ladders, pick them, and pack these oranges in neat rows in three-foot-deep wooden boxes, which get shipped around the country and sold year round.

The time passes and before I know it we're rounding the last corners before we reach our final destination. "Here comes the hill," my sister will yell, and my uncle will speed up, and over at high speed we will go. Our stomachs float to our heads and we all laugh and laugh. We arrive, the big Suburban rounding the sharp curve into the narrow cement driveway that *tio* Maike and *tio* Abel built last summer. The deserted park where the neighborhood dogs brawl is dry and yellow as usual. My grandma's generic mailbox wilts on its wooden post.

Woody, my grandma's dog, looks up from his shady spot, apathetically, too tired to move his head more than an inch. The doghouse my grandpa made out of leftover pieces of wood is still solid; the name WOODY is scrawled on it halfheartedly in red spray paint. Woody's metal plate sits crookedly in front; it has probably been run over a few times. He is one of the few lucky dogs to have survived traffic in the area. We have learned not to get attached to my grandma's dogs, as they come and go quickly.

My uncle parks the Suburban right in front of the house, which my three uncles and my grandpa built a few years back. Knowing nothing really about architecture, just stuff they learned here and there, they built the house up. They used any wood they could find at times, and improvised here and there. It may not be the perfect design for a house, but it serves its purpose and that is all that matters.

From behind the house my three cousins, Joaquin, Yesena, and Olgita, come running, one after the other. Joaquin, the oldest, nine, is always being tormented by these two little five-year-olds. Joaquin sees us, brushes his hair down, pulls up his jeans, and yells at the girls. We have so much to say to each other, it's been so long. His sad, big eyes look up at us with joy, maybe relief, to see my sister and me. We take some of the little kids off his back. My parents unload; I hug my other two cousins. Olgita, with her pudgy cheeks and fair skin, comes running after her brother, Joaquin. And Yesena, always the shy one, takes her time getting to know me again.

All smile as we wipe our muddy feet and go inside. I'm worried about my Spanish and what I will say to my grandma. If Mama Maria is feeling well, she will come to the iron screen door and smile, welcoming us. Having only been standing outside for a minute, we will be happy to enter the cool air-conditioned house. She is always more aged but she is still as sharp and witty as ever. Her arthritis prevents her from opening her hands, but they are always just right for fitting my hand in hers. I can always see how happy Mama Maria is to see my mom. Her whole body relaxes and embraces my mom with a huge hug.

Mama Maria's cockatiels chirp and flap their wings. We'll set our things in the living room/hallway and immediately head to the kitchen. It is a small room with many chairs so as to accommodate anyone and everyone who comes to visit. At times there won't be any chairs left. My *tio* Gustavo and my *tio* Abel love the big purple swivel chairs, which they are always fighting over. Figures, they are the biggest babies in the family. In general, my grandma's house is where all the family keeps in touch and hangs out together. Since my grandfather passed away, everyone comes up on the weekends to keep my grandma company and make sure her health is good. At Christmas the house is jam-packed. Most of our time is spent hanging out in the hot kitchen with the scent of tamales, *menudo,* fresh tortillas, *chorizo con huevo,* a pot of beans, and all sorts of good Mexican food, catching up and reminiscing. The fan overhead creaks and I am afraid it's going to fall any minute, on my head.

All the kids—me, my sister, Joaquin, Yesena, Olgita, Rene, Marqui, Delia, sometimes more—we hang out in the living room next to the dining room. In the small living room my grandma has a huge TV. And my cousin has all the latest Nintendo games. The sounds of people laughing and talking, food frying, shrieking toddlers, and Street Fighter mingle throughout the house. It's a makeshift house that is just right for our large family. Of course there aren't always enough beds.

I have a makeshift bed on the floor in the living room/hallway; my ears face the front porch where the rooster serves as an alarm to us all, especially me, at the crack of dawn. The rooster followed by, as always, my *tio* Abel's humongous snore, me and my "dog ears," as my family calls them. This is how I will spend my days and nights here at my grandma's. Here in the heart of the San Joaquin Valley, the part that no one sees when they pass. A place filled with wonderful people, culture, and most important, my family.

Moving away from home is always incredibly difficult. I was fourteen when my family moved to a large, diverse city; and on the hot August day we headed out of town, I was sure my life as I knew it had ended. I was positive I would never adjust. But, of course, I made friends, got involved in activities, and had many new experiences. And, as it turned out, moving was truly a gift—I just didn't know it at the time.

In "Away from Home," Ashley describes a move much more difficult than mine, one that involves an entirely new culture. Relocating from Singapore to America must have been extremely hard and emotionally straining. Ashley went through a rough transition, and although it may not be over yet, I'm glad that she is enjoying the United States more and hope that she finds happiness wherever she is.

AWAY FROM HOME

Ashley Sng, 13
ASIAN

At first, when my mom brought up the matter of relocating to America because of her job, I did not take the issue seriously. I knew it was impossible that we would move away from our beloved country.

But one day when we were having dinner in a nearby restaurant, she told us that we would have to move. Mixed feelings of fear and worry came over me. I had lived in Singapore for twelve whole years! This was all too sudden and shocking for me. Even though I tried my best to hold my tears and I really hated crying, tears started to fall, rolling uncontrollably down my cheeks, and my parents tried to console me.

They thought I was vexed about being in a new school and told me I could start school a little later. Being in a new school? That was the least of my worries. My relatives, my friends, and my best pal, Emily, the food, my favorite television programs, and most of all, my home—I have to leave all of them behind. Why did this have to happen? Of all the people in the world, why me? The thought of living in a foreign place was simply too overwhelming to bear.

A foreign place with a different culture, a different lifestyle, a different environment, and different people. What will the people in my new school think of me? Will they treat me differently just because I am Asian? Just because I look different? I was apprehensive about that, apprehensive about making friends. That night, I tried not to think about it, but I tried so hard that I could not get it off my mind. Moving kept haunting me like a heavy stone in my heart.

We made all the final arrangements—getting exempted from school, filing the necessary paperwork for our dog, making decisions on what to do with our house in Singapore, etc. On Saturday night, the day before our leave, I threw a farewell party and invited my closest friends. My friends were happy for me, as we had all read stories and watched movies of American life but had never had the chance to experience it firsthand. We had so much fun and when it was time for them to go, there were hugs and good-byes. We cheered up when I said I would be back soon.

When all our relatives saw us off at the airport, my mother was crying with all her sisters. However, I smiled sweetly at all my relatives, and my family headed toward the departure gate. I seemed okay outside and I did not even shed a tear, but deep inside, I really felt miserable.

While sitting by the window seat on the plane, I took a last glimpse of that little island, Singapore, my home, as the plane soared in the crimson sunset sky. I smiled sadly while sweet memories flashed across my mind. I never knew it could be so difficult to say good-bye. Good-bye, Singapore. It's time for me to experience another kind of life.

I thought a stay in America could be promising, with a lot of good things to come. There would certainly be many hardships and obstacles that could be overcome, however, with perseverance and determination. As it turned out, the first few months of life in America were terrible. My dad was not used to American food, my brother missed his friends, my mom thought of her family all the time, and I was quiet and reserved at school. It was ever so hard to make friends; it could have been because I felt I was different, that I was Asian. I used to dread going to school.

The most important subjects in school were math, science, English, and history. All these subjects were so different and I had trouble catching up. There were so many problems with school that I tolerated. I want to go home, I thought every time I went home from school and looked at myself in the mirror. Brown almond eyes, dark Asian hair . . . all these Asian features. Sometimes I really wished I were born American. That way I could fit in easily with the people here and that way I could understand the subjects in school. But the fact is, I am not an American. I am an Asian and I am proud of it.

We went back home to Singapore for the school holidays, and I was ecstatic. We went back in early November instead of December, as we could not wait. I got the chance to see our relatives, enjoy the food, and go back to school. However, when we returned to America, we spent our Christmas night at home like any other day, just the four of us—my parents, my brother, and me. I did not get any presents and we did not have our usual family gathering or exchange of presents like we did every other year. Since we did not have any relatives with us, we did not get to celebrate a Merry Christmas.

Months have passed so rapidly. I will be going to high school soon for my freshman year and possibly go back home to Singapore when I am a sophomore. Things are looking up now. School is okay as I am settled comfortably into my daily routine. The worst is over, and the problems I had are not as bad as before. I still miss my friends, but I have new ones. I call my best friend every week and e-mail my friends about the life here. They constantly ask when I will return and wait impatiently for that day to come. My dad found the food here not too bad, as there are Asian restaurants, and my mom chats on the Internet with her family now and then. As for my brother, he is doing fine and often e-mails his friends as well.

Being in America, I have discovered my passion for art, writing, and drama, which I had never had the opportunity to find while I was in Singapore. However, one valuable lesson I have learned is what the famous African American, Martin Luther King, Jr., said, "We should not be judged by the color of our skin but by the content of our character." I should not be concerned about racial identity, whether we are Caucasians, African Americans, or even Asians. Deep in our hearts, we are all the same and race does not matter at all. I am not certain when I will be able to return to Singapore, but one thing is for sure—no matter where I go, no matter what I do, I will always be the person I am inside.

Sia's piece took my breath away and left me in tears. The loss of her childhood, the transformation of her country, and the horrors of war she describes are things many of us would have trouble even imagining. Sia shares with us not only her own pain but that which she feels for her country, Sierra Leone.

Sia's teacher, Aurelia Blake, told me that Sia moved to the United States with family members in May 2000, from a refugee camp in Gambia. She says Sia is a beautiful woman with much spiritual strength, and that when there is peace, she hopes to return to Sierra Leone and become a nurse. I am thankful to Sia for sharing this piece and I admire her courage and endurance.

OUR STREET

Sia J. Yobah, 19

AFRICAN

When I was nine years old our street was full of life. During the dry season, December to June, our street was dusty. Our street was lined with houses of cinder block painted blue. Behind the houses women and children kept gardens of corn, tall as trees, green cassava leaves, and hot peppers. Cars passed and raised dust. The brown children playing in the street were always dirty, dusted beige.

When it was time to go home, we took our showers on the outside of the house. Sometimes the sun would have heated the water, almost to scalding. Women, men, it didn't matter, the dust had to come off. Cleanliness was more important than privacy.

Up and down the street, adults and children rode bikes. Bikes were transportation, not toys. We didn't buy toys. But when my father moved to the United States, he sent me Barbie dolls. But even before the store-bought toys, we made our toys. We made dolls with hair to braid.

The dry season was the time for weddings. Sometimes, there would be so many cars on a street, and people dancing, clapping, and singing in the street, no one could get through. Who would want to pass by without stopping to eat and celebrate the wedding of strangers or family alike? The colors of the dresses were like rainbows on fire.

It didn't matter if it was the rainy season or dry, we spent most of our days outside. We walked everywhere. We walked to school. We walked to market with containers of water, bundles of clothes, even baskets of vegetables balanced on our heads. Everywhere we walked, we talked. Even at night, groups of girls and boys walked to the homes of friends and cousins, to the soccer fields, the movie theater, or to the place where dancers and drummers met on street corners.

With my friends, older cousins, and classmates, I'd roam the streets, sometimes even until midnight. Even if I would get home late and my uncle would beat me, I didn't care. It was worth it. We would laugh, talk, sing, and dance everywhere, anywhere. The town was our town, our world, and the world was good.

But worlds can change and just as you can hear a storm coming, you can hear change.

It started with the arrival of people. Refugees from a war in another country began blowing into town like dead leaves, more blowing in every day. The importers and businesspeople began leaving the country.

Then they came. The Rebels, boys dressed in vests and shorts. The vests had been specially boiled in traditional medicine, giving the Rebels special protection. On their heads they tied a piece of red fabric. It came to mean, "We are here to kill people."

Now we have no right to speak about freedom of speech. The joy is gone. The suffering of young people today in our country is bad. Since the war began, I feel as if my childhood was a dream.

Our country has been at war since I was nine years old. Our brothers have been forming groups to kill people, taking away young girls and boys under the age of seven and forcing them to join their gangs. The children have one choice. They can join or they will be killed.

In 1987, the winds of war started blowing out of Liberia. In 1990, the Rebels started another style of fighting in our street. Boys write words on a paper like a choice.

They would write "long sleeve," "short sleeve," and "one love." "Long sleeve" meant they would cut off your hand. "Short sleeve" meant your arm would be cut off above the elbow. "One love" meant you would lose all of your fingers, leaving only your thumbs. They would torture people, even newborn babies. With pregnant women, they would haggle back and forth over the sex of the baby. When they stopped, they would say, "Let's prove it." Then they would make the woman lie down flat, split her stomach, take the baby out, and start beating the baby.

This is the kind of situation where young girls and boys have not gone to school for many years. Even now, there is no good education in our country. I have not gone to school for four years because I've been moving to another place. Every few months or weeks the Rebels attacked places and found people. So if they attacked where we were, in the provinces, we would run away with no shoes or clothes in our hands. The last time they attacked us in the provinces, we tried to go to the city of Freetown. We finally made it. We arrived in Freetown and started going to school for a month and the Rebels attacked the city again.

We sat home, dressing like old women. We'd make ourselves dirty so we would not be recognized as young girls. Sometimes we wouldn't eat food for a week because we couldn't go outside of our house. We could not use our showers outside until after midnight. Sometimes, the Rebels came inside someone's house to look for food, girls, boys, and properties. At night they would come and wake everyone up with their guns to sing and clap for them. If you don't, you will die.

This is my street, my town, my world. The houses have been bombed. There are no more cars on the street. The grass has grown up taller than a man. There are no gardens, no street, no people, only rats and vultures.

Different cultures have always fascinated me. When my mother married my stepfather, we were transported into a different kind of culture. I was exposed to Lakota ceremonies and language. I began to attend wacipis *(powwows), and I even participated in the sweat lodge ceremony. My stepfather introduced me to a new kind of lifestyle, and I found it captivating. The most interesting thing I found was that his culture had been sustained, despite the destructive influence of the dominant culture. It amazed me that my stepfather was able to attend a traditional ceremony and then go to a movie at the Cineplex. This balance has proved to be difficult, but livable.*

So often it seems as if the United States demands that its inhabitants assimilate to the "American" culture. And it has always seemed to me that "American" has been synonymous with "white." People of varying backgrounds struggle to maintain their own cultures in the United States with much difficulty. I attend school with immigrants from Ethiopia and Sudan, and often wonder what they must think of American society.

Sneha's piece touches on something many of us are forced to deal with: balancing our individual cultures with the dominant one.

INDIAN ROOTS

Sneha Upadhyay, 17
ASIAN INDIAN

Just as I'm about to leave the house to meet my friends, my mom comes downstairs and says, "Can you please take your brother to his soccer game at two?" And then adds, "His haircut is right after that, and on your way back home, can you please pick up two gallons of milk?" I call my friends and tell them I'll be late, and then I take my brother. If I told my parents that I already had other plans, they would respond, "You don't do anything when we ask you to."

I've been in America since I was eight months old, and I have lived here with my parents, two siblings, and two grandparents. My parents are both from India, and they want me to practice the same culture as they did. However, the culture around me is the American culture. So the question is, Do I practice the culture of the society that surrounds me or should I exercise the Indian values as my parents taught me?

I try to think positively, put the good qualities of both cultures together, and create my own little world. My parents and I disagree on many subjects. First of all, in the Indian culture, education is the only goal of a teenager. Nothing should come in the way of success in that area. I understand my parents' point of view that education is the key to success, but I believe that life is too short to wait for happiness. My relationships with friends and their emotions are a big part of me. For example, last year, my little brother had his school concert, and the next day I had my chemistry test. I went to my brother's concert because it made him elated to see his sister there to support him. Another subject, which my parents and I disagree on, would be the gender issue. Here in America, having guy friends is normal for any teenage girl, but my parents have to know every little detail about the guy before he helps me with my homework. Finally, in India, one's family members are expected to live with you. Some families have everyone (including distant family members) in the same house. Here in America, a visit from the in-laws is a big fuss.

Even though it is hard to keep a balance between my friends and my family, I know that my family is my first priority. I've learned that no matter what happens in life, people need support systems. Sometimes, even the friends who they think will always be there for them aren't, and without the advice and friendship of their family, the struggling person would be lost. However, my belief was put to the test during my sophomore year of high school. My father's sister Smita, her husband, Mayu, and their young twin boys, Dip and Div, came to live with us for a year and a half. At first, I was extremely excited and couldn't wait for them to come. Before they came to the United States, I had no blood-related family members here. Before my relatives arrived, I told everyone they were coming, and I even agreed with my parents to allow them to use my room and bathroom while they were here. My cousins Dip and Div were adorable at first. Their curiosity struck me and made me realize how much technology we take for granted. For example, when my dad used the garage door opener, my cousins frantically hid behind a blanket because they thought the garage door had a ghost in it.

As time passed, however, the structure of my daily life slowly deteriorated. I couldn't talk to my parents without my aunt putting her opinion in the situation. The attention that my parents gave to me slowly slipped away. They had so much other work to do that they didn't really talk to me about my daily work. I had to sneak my way online late at night so I could talk to my best friend because my aunt would think negatively of me if she found out that I was talking to a boy. I was forced to eat Indian food most of the week because my cousins didn't like American food. Our van, which seats seven people, was now seating eleven. I didn't mind my aunt using my room, but it bothered me that she moved my furniture to suit her taste.

These problems were an annoyance to me. I never said anything about them, but they really bugged me. I started expressing myself only after they affected my studying. With eleven people in the house, it was difficult to study. I would walk through the house a million times telling people to be quiet and let me study, but daily chattering still continued. My goal is to do my best at whatever I do. I promised myself that if any interruptions came in my way, I would do anything I could to get out of that environment and put 110 percent of my focus back on my work. So, for most of the year, I came home from school at 3:30 P.M. and I went to the local library until it closed at 9:00 P.M. It was difficult because we only have two cars, and my parents both work so I had no transportation to get to the library. Most of the time, I would walk about three miles each way to and from the library with my book bag.

Even though the time with my extended family was chaotic, I learned many lessons I wouldn't have learned by just reading. I learned how to be patient with people, not to take what you have for granted, and how to think of others. It's been about two years since they moved out and they are happily settled out west. Since the move, I am much closer to them, and this summer, I'm going to India with my aunt and her family. All in all, the whole cultural experience taught me patience and how to accept other people.

Brittney's has written a heart-wrenching description of abandonment as seen through a young girl's eyes. It's almost impossible to read "Is This Love?" without wanting to comfort Brittney and let her know that it wasn't her fault. Although Brittney experienced much pain, I'm glad that she has resolved to someday become the kind of mother she always wanted.

IS THIS LOVE?

Brittney West, 17
AFRICAN AMERICAN

"She's coming," my dad keeps telling me, "she's coming." So I wait and wait, coat and gloves on, suitcase filled with toys and clothes ready to go. I keep clicking my heels together, thinking I could be like Dorothy in *The Wizard of Oz* or something, and magically my mommy would appear. "Come on, Mommy, come get me," I keep saying to myself. "I'm ready, why aren't you here?" Sometimes she is late. Other times she just doesn't come.

Every Friday since my parents' divorce I wait. I'll sit on the steps pushing back tears, hoping this time she'll come. I keep thinking if I leave, then she will see that I am not here and drive away. Is this love that I feel? I don't know. My daddy says for me to come on back in the house, but I can't. I'm not worried about getting cold or frostbitten, only the worry that Mommy will not come. I lie on the porch with my dolls and sing them a song. Finally I just cry myself to sleep. I'm too stiff and hurt to move and my Daddy comes and picks me up. His strong black hands lift me on his shoulders and take me to my bed. He removes my coat buttoned so tight and unties my shoes. He puts on my nightie and kisses my cheek.

It has happened again, another Friday Mommy doesn't come, another broken heart. Mommy will call Saturday as usual and make up some story as to why she wasn't there, and promise to be there next time, and for some reason I believe her. After she gets off the phone with me I can hear my daddy telling her she can't continue doing this and that he doesn't know what to say anymore. He knows of his only child's broken heart but yet does not know how to mend it. I hear him telling her how I cry myself to sleep and how she needs to be more responsible. "Don't you want to be in her life, don't you want to see her grow up?" And then the phone slams and there is silence. What has happened, is this love? I don't know. I constantly asked myself why do all my other friends have mommies, why do they get hugs and kisses and I love you's. It isn't fair.

I no longer wait for Mommy for she has stopped coming. In one more year I will be eighteen, and I haven't seen Mommy since I was five. I have a lot of things I want to ask and tell her. I want her to know about the boy I like at school, I want to compare our features to see if we look alike, I want her to braid my hair, I want her to help me pick out my prom dress, I want to have late-night talks about "women" stuff, I want her. There is that side of me that wants to punch her and make her feel all the pain I have felt. I want her to cry all the tears that flooded my pillow every night. I want her to feel not good enough. I always felt that if my own mom didn't love me, then who would? I felt rejection and wanted her to also. Was I not smart enough, pretty enough, nice enough? Can't she at least try to call? I feel this way, thinking, Is this love? I don't know. All I know is that when I have children they will not wait for me because I will be there. They will not cry guilty tears on pillows, not have to question what love is, they will know. I promise to be there every day of their lives.

"Through Those Articulate Eyes" describes the distance Sokonie feels between herself and her mother. I have always been very close to my mother, and so this piece makes me sad. It must be very painful to experience this kind of relationship within one's own family.

THROUGH THOSE ARTICULATE EYES

Sokonie S. Freeman, 18

AFRICAN

There's not really much to them. They're shaped like ovals, and are about one inch apart from each other. The whites are slightly tinted with just a touch of yellow and the irises are brown. Others may think my mother's eyes are just the standard brown eyes, but they're wrong. Her eyes are powerful; through them I know her. I have been hurt, saved, and on some occasions loved through these eyes.

My mother's eyes function like the inside of a computer. One glance from them is like a hundred tiny, electronic codes. When I was younger, from about the age of four to six, when she would return from one of her three- to four-month disappearances, she would squat down before me, look into my confused eyes, and in my left hand place some loose change: shiny quarters, dimes, and pennies—as if those bright, jangly coins could make up for all that she had deprived me of. Her gestures tried to silently persuade me to believe that everything was just as they should be, but her dependable eyes, as they always do, gently whispered the unfortunate truth—and I accepted it.

With my mother's self-absorbed love, she was always traveling, leaving me in the care of my grandmother or anybody else who happened to be around. By the time she made the decision to finally settle down and take responsibility for the child she had brought into the world, it was too late, at least for me. My mother and I rarely engage in affectionate contact or converse about casual subjects, and we never, never let the commonly used three-word phrase that generally passes between parents and their offspring roll off our tongues. If that were to happen, we would feel as if we had just ripped layers and layers of clothing off of our bodies and exposed ourselves to the entire world—too afraid that the uncomfortable feeling would remain permanent. So we live, breathe, and function in the same household, my mother using only her eyes to serve as messengers of true communication from her to me.

Those two brown, almond-shaped messengers are not always the bearers of bad news, though. There have been certain occasions when they have let me see my mother in a way that few people see their mothers. In my times of harsh fevers, she sat me in cold water and gently poured cool water over my suffering body with a plastic cup. Her sincere eyes then seemed to say a prayer, "Lord, please deliver my child." From this look, seeing that she wanted me alive, I was saved. Then there have been times when she would look at me, even today, and her eyes would penetrate beyond my flesh, aiming directly at my heart and continually apologize, "I'm sorry . . . I'm sorry . . . I'm sorry."

I wish I could tell her, "No need to be sorry, Fate has a weird way of working." Oh, if I could just say, "It's not your fault, this is the plan of a Divine Being." For her eyes have told me this is not how she wants to be; now she searches for change. Every morning she awakes, indulges herself in a hot shower, picks out one of her decorative scrubs, and irons it. After dressing, she goes to the mirror and makes up every inch of her face, being very careful to put as little as possible around her eyes. She tells me, "You never know whom you're going to run into when you get out there," but her eyes tell me different. Before entering her world, she is desperate and hopes that everybody will be deceived by her pleasant-smelling body and beautiful attire and not notice her eyes, which reveal her aching heart; she glances one last time in the mirror. She uses this strategy often because she has found that it works. People usually see her as she appears, but knowing that she can never hide from herself, she constantly moves about, always proclaiming, "I'm busy, I'm busy," fearing that if she were to ever stop for just one moment, she would be forced to probe her life and realize where Fate has led her.

I remember the day her eyes revealed great pain. She was a dark figure lying horizontally across her unmade bed with her face buried in a pillow. From the open doorway where I stood as a nine-year-old, my body resting on the cold, wood frame, I could see the soft, subtle movements of her shoulders and back, and hear the silent moaning of her voice. Staring into the dark room, clenching on to a damp washcloth, I remember that I couldn't see her eyes, but I imagined that they were probably bloodshot, moist, and puffy. Had she broken her daily routine of keeping "busy"? What in this world was so significant and powerful to have gotten her to stop and think? When I finally walked in the room to hand her the washcloth, she took it without the faintest movement of her head or body, only her arm. I stood there for just a second more before turning and leaving the room. She never told me then what was wrong, it was only later that I learned she was grieving because my grandmother, her mother, had fallen ill in Africa. She just couldn't share that pain with me. In her eyes, I was a child who had never experienced the special bond between a mother and her daughter; therefore, I couldn't relate to her situation.

I have often wondered how those eyes reacted when they first rested upon me. Did they look at me with warm adoration? Were they grateful for the gift that was bestowed upon them? I'll bet those eyes reflected, instead, a scared eighteen-year-old girl, a girl who didn't know what she was going to do with a child, or how she was going to even attempt to take care of it. The setting is different now; her eyes have matured; now they search for all the things that they had previously run away from. They search for love, courage, stability, and even the child they once feared. My only hope and prayer for her is that she finds and possesses all of these things someday. I will keep praying and hoping, because heaven knows I want this for her as badly as she does—perhaps even more—sometimes I wish she would let me speak to her through my caring eyes.

Amisha's piece is simply beautiful. It artfully describes her village, her family, and her feelings. As it begins Amisha writes of a dream, and throughout the entire piece she continues to describe her life in Ugat as though it were a dream, filled only with fun, beauty, and happiness. Sometimes I think of my childhood this way. Although it did not take place in a setting as picturesque as Ugat, my days were often filled with fun, beauty, and happiness, too. Amisha's piece is about her village in India, but it's also about the dreamy existence of a happy child.

UGAT: MY VILLAGE IN INDIA

Amisha Padhair, 13
INDIAN

Sleep in Ugat is like a transformation from one dream world to another. The burst of glowing Indian sun through opening curtains slowly lifts me out of my dreams. The first touch of cold tiles underneath my feet jolts me into reality and brings my senses tumbling back from my previously dreamy state. The bedroom looks so still, as if it were a picture painted on a stretch of canvas.

As I step out of my room, scattering butterflies stream out in the chaos of opening doors after the still cool of a moonlit night. The world is abuzz with life. My cousins and I pitter-patter down the stairs. Our charm-covered anklets and bangles fill the cavernous but love-filled home with sweet, innocent jingling.

Our mothers are in the kitchen with Grandma. The kitchen is ablaze with the aura of motherly love. The aroma of spicy Indian curry, whose tastes dance on your tongue, exhilarating you with a world full of rich flavors, floats out of the kitchen doors. The warm glow bursting from the burning fire makes shadows dance upon the soft, clay walls.

My mother spots me and shuffles me into the bathroom for a bath. Stepping into the wind after a steaming, refreshing bath feels like reincarnation.

Walking upstairs, to my bedroom, I stop to touch the slowly peeling paint of my Bapa's bungalow. Hiding behind it are thirty years of memories and times. If I look closely, I can still see my Bapa's face, smiling right back at me, from beneath it.

After getting ready, I rush over the steaming sands of our dusty brown road, past the many clay homes with a story hidden in each one, over to the hills of my village. The grass hills of Ugat seem like a rich, green cloak of silk laid on the sandy, white skin of an angel. And there, amidst this heaven on earth, lies my swing, my cloud of dreams laid in the halo of the angel.

As I begin to swing, I forget all my worries. As the wind weaves through my hair, the swing transforms into my pair of wings and carries me high. I sweep through the crisp, cuddling air and soar far into the deep ocean blue sky. My *oodhni* (scarf) trails behind me, creating a vivid flock of butterflies, which dance through my open locks of mesmerizing, midnight black, at the slightest change of wind. I am lost amidst my thoughts for hours, and then I step out of this dream world and begin to walk home.

Walking down an open road, during the hour before the setting sun, I am caught by the fields which dance across the never-ending lands. The fields of Ugat seem like gold and green emeralds placed in the dark brown hair of a sly and sleek Egyptian princess. They seem to call me closer and I simply cannot resist. The ripening corn stalks whisper to me in the dark voice of the wind while I run and play amongst them. The moist soils cuddle my feet while I chase a leaf through the muddy, wet, and luscious rice fields. And finally, as Mother Nature pastels the sky and sends the sun home after a day of play, I reach home also. The bed greets me at the end of the day as a mother calling her child for a long and comforting hug. The covers wrap around me as if to say that I will forever be protected by the purity that lies in a good night's sleep. One glance out the window shows the moon. A familiar, yet unknown face, a face of the future, is hidden deep inside the coolness of midnight moon and clouds.

The slow ticking of the grandfather clock cuts into the night's silence like a warmed knife cuts through a cool block of butter. And finally, the warm darknesses behind closed eyes engulf me. I slip off into another dream world, another magnificent utopia.

Taia submitted two pieces—one showcasing her father's strengths and the other his weaknesses. In the beginning I planned to use one piece, because although they were both well written, I felt the messages were contradictory. However, I liked them both, and the more I thought about it, the more I wanted to include both. So I decided to call Taia.

When I spoke with Taia, she told me of the closeness she felt to her father and the confusion she felt when she saw what he did. The combination of these two pieces describes something I think that many of us can relate to—a struggle between love and anger. When I talked to her, I asked her if she was happy now. She said she is, and that her parents are divorced and also happier.

DADDY'S GIRL

Taia Waltjen, 16

HAWAIIAN

"Stop looking at me with those puppy dog eyes!" I grunt, a smile playing on my lips. "What puppy dog eyes?" the scoundrel counters, trying his best to execute a serious expression. "Those ones!" I shoot back, pointing at him accusingly. As he laughs, his body jerks with pleasure at my frustration. "How do you want me to look at you then?" Portraying every last facial expression imaginable, he tests me wickedly. Weakly, I give out a chuckle in small amusement. "Oh, Dad, you are exhausting!" I finally sigh, shaking my head.

A typical father-daughter conversation? I think not. My dad and I have always been close. For example, who was the one to give me the talk about the birds and the bees? Although he didn't explain it in the most tactful way, he got the general idea across. It took up every last ounce of courage to finally release the truth to me, the virtuous sixth-grader. Because he had made the effort, I decided to be oblivious to the idea (even if I had learned everything there was to know in the fifth grade). I decided to give him brownie points, no matter how pathetic the lesson. I guess that was something he felt obligated to do, and I didn't want him to feel as if he had neglected one of his parental responsibilities.

Who taught me to tame the beast of pavement? My father had been the one to remove the training wheels from my bike. He had been the one running alongside me every day, chanting, "You can do it, just keep on pedaling!" He gave me the motivation to keep going and soon I had gotten the hang of it.

Who could accomplish the most inhumane punishments—the silent treatment and the disappointed glance? He was the one to make me sink in my seat. He found the places where it hurt the most and used them to his advantage. He had also mastered reverse psychology and didn't need to resort to spanking. He did discipline me, don't get me wrong, but I have no hard feelings toward him. I understand that he had just been trying to protect and teach me the way he had been taught.

With distance making communication a little more difficult, we still manage to retain our special bond. I tell my father everything— from the new sociology assignment to the hunks in the sociology course—I bare all. Sometimes I think I reveal a little too much because he ends up sighing weakly. I enjoy putting a few gray hairs on his head. That's why I am so proud to say that he's mine. Despite all the agony I along with my sisters put him through, his love remains constant and unchanging.

In many ways, he serves as a hero for me. He is the ultimate hard-working, crime-fighting, protector of the innocent. To this day, I still can't understand how he can manage a family, of eight—six of them being females! If anyone had any impact on my life, it would have to be him—his drive, his passion for his family, and his drive for providing the best for his loved ones. If you're listening to this, Dad, I love you.

LIFE'S LESSONS

Quivering and insecure, I forced my unreliable arm down to better steady my grip on the glass of water and lowered the corn bread with the other. Looking up from the television nervously, I glanced back at the area where I had last seen my parents. A loud slam on the table had startled my sisters and me from our cartoon video, *Once Upon a Forest*. We all reluctantly looked back in time to see a child-sized cup of fruit punch dance furiously on the kitchen floor. The red liquid formed the misshapen shadow of a large butter-fly. Neither the dance nor the beautiful creature would have ever been thought to have been formed by such a grim explosion. We were agitated when we noticed my mother crying and my father glaring accusingly with daggers in his eyes. I forced a choked gulp of corn bread down my throat—perhaps believing that if I continued to ignore the situation it would go away. It didn't. Again I forced another gulp of the food down; this time it was moist and salty, drenched by my river of tears. As the ironic, depressing mood music played from the television, I took note that the little gopher's parents had died in a tragic accident. I quickly swept up my sisters in my tiny arms and guided them to one of the back rooms. I paced the room for a while, trying to organize the rush of thoughts in my mind. My sisters huddled in the corner, wide-eyed and afraid. I marveled at my control—where had that flash of courage come from? As I gazed into the eyes of my two-year-old sister, innocent and torn, the answer came to me immediately. I acted upon the fearful realization that the scenario was hurting my siblings. I gathered up just enough strength to defend them.

I recall this scene so vividly. It is strange to have such detailed remembrances of an unhappy past. The scenario continued further into more heartache and more tears after I left my sisters, speaking in a comforting and reassuring tone. I returned to the horrible scene to find my dad yelling at my mom for her transgression. My dad hit her and with his blow, he hit me in my heart. It was physically evident that our happy family would never be the same. While my mom's muffled cries instructed me to call the police, my dad yelled not to. That was the greatest mental struggle I had ever had. I had to abide by either my mother's pleas or my father's demands. I was afraid of what my father would do if I didn't call but realized that it might be even worse to aggravate the situation, so I cried in confusion and slumped against the wall in a corner, helpless and upset.

Remarkably, I recovered from the incident. I was forced to understand at a young age the trials one faces through life. I learned not to expect the perfect family and that there was really nothing I could have done about it and that it wasn't my fault. I am proud to say that I have succeeded in surviving the most difficult time in my life; many teens do not survive divorce well, and I credit myself for handling it as well as I could.

As I compiled this book I soon noticed the lack of contributions addressing sexual orientation. I felt this was a very important topic and needed to be discussed. I contacted gay and lesbian organizations requesting that they give information on the book to any teenage girls of color. I also asked friends of mine to write about how society treats homosexual, bisexual, and transgender people; personal experiences; and how they themselves feel about being lesbian, bisexual, or heterosexual in a very heterosexual world. Still, I received nothing.

I was almost ready to give up when I received this piece from a young woman who wishes to remain anonymous. Although not solely focused on gay and lesbian issues, it does recognize how unfairly homosexual people are treated and how their oppression is similar to the racism people of color experience. By telling of her father's prejudice against blacks and gays, the author conveys how the treatment that both groups encounter is unfair and should not be tolerated.

The other reason I like this piece is the way in which the author questions her family's belief system and ends up affirming her own identity.

MY FAMILY

Anonymous, 15

HISPANIC

I'm fifteen years old. I am a girl of color who as a child was thought to be polite, nice, and well mannered. It was important in my family to say hello, thank you, bless you, good-bye, and to dress appropriately. My father, for example, would get mad if I asked him a question he thought was dumb or if he asked me to bring him something and I didn't know what he wanted. My father always told me that playing sports or games would never take me far but working would. He would always have bad feelings about gay or black people, because of his religion, he said, and his past in a bad neighborhood. My mother was always telling me what guy I should get, for example, not shorter than me, not darker than me, and he had to have a mustache. I remember how she used to put all these clothes on me and say, "My little doll."

I've never been able to talk to my parents about what I've learned about gay people, that they are not something to laugh at, but people who need support. Our religion might say that gay people never will enter heaven, but as I see it, the Spaniards brought that religion after conquering the Aztecs.

My family and friends have told me stories about how black people are not to be trusted with things and that they are bad people. That's not true. I've learned about racism and what black people have been through and how hard they have worked to get where they are today.

My family has affected me, but it's just an example I do not want to follow. You see, I cannot even tell my family what I like, who I like, or even speak up for myself on any occasion. My parents and family have always said that you cannot trust anybody, not even your pet.

But with the classes I have taken and with the help of some teachers, I have found out that I am important.

"Justice (for My Momma)" was probably the hardest piece to read of all those that I received. I found myself crying for Tara and for all of us who have made it through intensely painful experiences.

I chose not to put this story with the other stories of pain, sorrow, and death, because I felt that it had a different message—about the love and hatred associated with family.

Only sixteen, Tara has experienced more than many of us will in a lifetime. I wish to offer my support, love, and admiration for Tara. And Sister, I'm sure your mother is so proud.

JUSTICE (FOR MY MOMMA)

Tara Ashley Chaney, 16
AFRICAN AMERICAN / KOREAN

Imagine everything you know in this world being taken away from you. In an instant your life would change and there would be no way to get it back. I have lived like this, day after day, dealing with the loss of my mother and the sick realities of life.

My dad was taken away when I was around fourteen. I still can feel his presence in our house. He was the most vicious man I had ever met. We called him Dice because that's what his life became—a big game of dice, always hustling and hoping to win, never stopping even when he lost.

My mom met him in high school and she thought he was everything she ever wanted. They were together three months before she got pregnant with me. It all started good. They owned a small apartment, had a little money, and were really happy together. Soon jobs became scarce and nobody would hire him. He had been earning money the only way he could . . . getting in trouble. He once thought about leaving town because he was caught selling drugs and stealing. His theory was that the police wouldn't arrest a family man so he stuck around a little longer. Things started getting bad between him and my mom. He started hitting her and bringing street women over to the house. It became an everyday thing for him. But Momma didn't care. She thought one day he would fall in love with one of them and leave her but it never happened.

I knew she was sick of life but wouldn't give up. She knew that she couldn't get away from him. She once tried, but he found her in the back room packing with me right there on the bed, seven months old. He was drunk and started to hit her, and he said that if she ever tried stuff like that again, he would kill her. After that she was too scared to leave.

Sometimes I would go into her room at night when I heard her cry. She would always say not to worry about her because she would be okay. She was just sorry for how we lived and what she kept putting me through. I understood. Because I was sorry, too.

"Baby," she would say. "Imma get you outta here soon, real soon." But for some reason I didn't believe her. I knew she was too scared.

Through the years my mother and I grew really close. We had to because it seemed like we only had each other. Nobody else could understand us. We were too ashamed to tell anybody outside of the family what Dice did to us so we kept it to ourselves. She had become my best friend; we were inseparable. Sometimes we would pile in her old raggedy car—it was probably two seconds away from breaking down—and ride around town like we were the queens of Africa visiting all of our townspeople. When we would get home we would laugh for hours at the crazy things we did that day. She loved to laugh.

She reminded me of my granny, always warm, looking on the bright side of things, trying not to show me any pain, always keeping me happy even when she wasn't. Her face was always bright and flawless. The prettiest eyes in the world were placed there. Her skin was dark and healthy, her lips reminded me of a peach, and she smelled like summer and happiness. "Don't ever give up," she would say. "Make good choices and don't settle for anything less than you deserve. Don't marry another Dice . . . Lord knows, that's the last thing I need." Then she would smile. She tried to always be happy around me but when Dice came around I could see the pain in her eyes.

One day when I came home from school I saw the door to our house open. That was really weird because Dice was a well-known drug dealer and crack fiend along with being a thief. He always said that if he caught us leaving the door open then he would do something crazy. My mom's car was parked out back in the storage area. She was usually home around this time. She never left me home alone with him. I didn't understand. I went in very cautiously and aware of everything. There were broken lamps, shattered glass, beer bottles, and all my mother's things were gone. So were Dice's. At first I thought that he had just given one of those street women all of Momma's clothes and had left with her. I started to smile, thinking of how happy Momma would be and the fun we would have.

I heard someone in the house. It sounded like someone was crying and saying help at the same time. I rustled through all of the broken things trying to find where the noises were coming from. I knew I was getting closer because the words began to get clearer and clearer.

"Help! Help! Somebody." It was an odd and weary sound that filtered through the air. I kept on going toward the noise and with every step my heart began to sink deeper and deeper into my chest. I began to think of all the possibilities of what the sound might be. Then I saw her: Momma had bruises all over her face, she was in a bed of her own blood. She just lay, making an effort to look happy, with tears running down her cheeks.

"Aw baby . . ." she barely choked out. "How ya doing? I didn't want you to find me like this." She paused, gasping for air, "Got to call 911 . . . Momma is hurt and I need some help." The look of desperation on her face grew as the words came from her mouth. She tried to smile but the pain was too great.

I turned around to get the phone. I could barely hit the buttons because I was shaking so much. Over and over I asked myself, why did this happen to her? The operator asked me questions and I tried my best to answer but it was hard. It was about twenty minutes until the ambulance and police came. I don't know why it took so long as the hospital and police station are around the block. They loaded my mother and me into the ambulance and rushed off. She was really quiet and had her head turned away from me. I guess it was for the best. I didn't want to see in her face the pain she had to go through. They rushed us into an emergency room.

I waited and waited and waited. Every minute I waited it scared me more and more. Thoughts ran through my head continuously of what the outcome would be. It was about twenty to thirty minutes before a doctor came out and pronounced her dead. I don't know how I reacted, to tell the truth. I must have fainted because when I got up doctors were all around me putting me in a bed, screaming at each other, "Where is her father! Somebody call him."

"No! No!" I cried, trying to get out of the bed. They just kept holding me down.

Everyone began to back away and look at me. "Hey, sweetie, I am Nurse Carpenter. Now why don't you want us to call your daddy?" A tall woman stood above me. She looked trustworthy and sweet; her smile gave me comfort and reminded me of my mother's.

"Look Makia, she's not going to talk; she is in shock." The doctor beside me whispered in Nurse Carpenter's ear and acted as if I couldn't hear him.

"Robert, look, I want her to be with someone whom she feels content around, just back away please . . . let me do my job!" With that, Nurse Carpenter grabbed my hand and took me into one of the empty rooms across the hall. "I'm going to let you rest awhile while we get this whole thing settled. If you need me I'll be across the hall."

I waited for a while, sitting on the bed at first, but the hospital room began to get to me. There was a knock at the door. It was Nurse Carpenter. "Hey, sweetie, are you ready to go down to the police station so they can write up a report?"

I nodded my head.

"We tried to call your father but he wasn't home." She acted like I actually cared. I hated him. I never wanted to talk to him again.

The drive to the police station was long. I kept replaying what might have happened to my mother while I was gone and imagining the things I would do to Dice if I ever saw him again. I was too mad to cry. In a way I was still hoping that she would come back, laughing and telling me that it was just a joke.

The officer who drove me to the station told me to wait because the psychologist hadn't arrived.

That's when I saw Dice charging me like a wild bull. That's when it began to register—he took my mother away from me, he beat her, he killed her. He was the one who caused her to cry at night. I knew it and that's all I needed.

When he came close enough I started punching, scratching, and pulling on him and cursing his name and saying how much I hated him. There were about four policemen on me, finally pulling me off him. I was still trying to escape from them and attack Dice.

He just stood there looking at me for a while with a smile on his face. "Oh, you want to fight, huh?" I could smell the weed and alcohol on his breath. "Well, I can't leave without a fair fight." He began to walk around, and when he was halfway out of the door he turned around and charged toward me, tackling me to the ground, hitting me over and over, banging my head on the ground, beating me like I was a rag doll. I felt blood starting to come from my head. My body went numb and I couldn't feel a thing. It took about ten guards to get him off me. They immediately took him to a cell, without reading him his rights or anything. Then they called a doctor to check me out. I had minor injuries to the head and they said I went into shock. The police decided that they didn't want to put me through any more emotional stress so I was asked if I had any close relatives whom I would like to stay with. I told them that I wanted to go to my grandmother's house.

When she arrived at the police station she had a Bible in one hand and a cross in the other. At the first sight of me she threw her arms around me, saying that the Lord had saved me from the devil himself.

Grandma Williams was my mom's mom. Every time I looked at her it made me want to cry. They looked so much alike. I could see through her smile the pain she was going through. I knew how she felt. She looked like she had been crying for years straight.

That night I couldn't go to sleep. I kept thinking about my mom, how things were never going to be the same. I had never imagined living life without her. I looked into the sky, searching for her face in the clouds watching over me. "Momma, why did this happen? We were supposed to be together forever. Momma, I can't live without you." I buried my face in my arms, and tears streamed down my face. I looked back up into the sky, seeing that nobody was there. Nobody was watching over me. No face, no Momma. The reality of everything came together. She was gone and nothing could bring her back. I promised her and myself that night that I would get Dice back even if it took me the rest of my life. He would regret hurting us.

The morning came when my grandmother told me that I had a court date tomorrow. She smiled at me. "Baby, do what you have to do to make your momma proud." That's all she had to say.

I had waited forever for this day to come. I walked inside of the courtroom with my head held high and ready to put Dice where he should be. It was six hours of long questioning and painful testimony that reminded me of my mother. I tried not to cry. I didn't want Dice to see my pain. He just sat there looking drunk and lost like always.

He didn't even look sorry. When he got up to give his testimony, he had the nerve to lie and said that he loved her too much to even think about hitting her. I could hear the angry voices of her family talking under their breath. I could tell that even his attorney didn't have faith in him after that. We had a short recess while the jury decided on the case. Coming back, I had a weird feeling that he would get off as usual. I tried to let it go but I knew that he had always gotten away before.

"Will the court rise for the honorable Judge Hewitt." We all stood, nervous and unsure.

The only word I heard was "guilty." I got up on the table and held my hands up, thanking the Lord that justice was done. Outbursts of joy filled the room.

As we went outside, news cameras were everywhere. "Any last words you would like to say?" a reporter asked.

I looked at her. "Momma, this is for you. He's gone forever!"

When I first read Shivani's story, I didn't know why she'd written about her mother. I then realized that as Shivani learned about her mother she learned about herself. She was able to imagine her mother's struggles and thus connect more with her mother and with her own struggles. By understanding her mother's life, she was slowly unveiling her own. Shivani's writing helps us all remember that our mothers' histories are part of our own lives.

SILENT SOLDIER

Shivani Agarwal, 17
INDIAN

He shuffles through the plaques and the envelopes marking his successful departure: red seals, bleached sheets of heavy paper, black writing—on the right, the words tell me his accomplishments in the language I know, and on the left, they speak in a language aching to be revived by my tongue. After searching through more drawers, he finally finds hers, tucked away into the dark depths of the drawer, a thick piece of paper with cream-colored corners creased by neglect. In the middle is a black smudge, probably a mistake made by the writer of the degree who was too careless to use a new sheet. Her name is written there in ink, into the history of the class of 1975, signed by a distant dean who shakes her hand and smiles with that look of faint interest.

My mother still can't believe the news that came to her that boiling summer day. The moist air had steamed open the envelope for her and while she sat on the front step reading that word "accepted" over and over again until it was ingrained in her head, her family prepared a celebration dinner with all of her favorite dishes. That night, her mother let her sleep on the roof under the yawning sky. Her mother sang to her, as is the custom in our family. "For you, I have decided to sing a song that I have not sung to you since you were a small child. This way, you can remember me." So my mother listened as her mother reminisced about those moments in my mom's childhood that she did not want to let go of, memories of her and her mother in the garden and in the kitchen and on the roof.

Sometimes I try to picture this moment when they were at the top of their world. Except this time, I'm my mom and my mom is hers. She sings the beautiful song to me in her native tongue with smooth notes and unwavering words. She has "butterflies on her tongue" they say, when someone's song is as beautiful as the image of a butterfly in flight. Often, I wish I had butterflies on my tongue.

At the All India Institute, there were so many rules. The gates didn't open until 8:00 in the morning for classes, but my mother never paid attention to this. She and her two girlfriends would get up at 5:00, when the sun was just beginning to show itself, and climb over the tall iron gates to the pool. After a refreshing swim, she and her friends went to the dining hall. Breakfast was already set for them; it was always the same: a slice of bread and fried eggs, half an orange, and a small glass of milk. Their classmates always whispered and snickered at them. "Look, they always have drenched hair when they come to class, not like our girls at home who are always so smart-looking." "Clearly," she would say, "they were just jealous that we could always get away with sneaking in every morning."

In class, she was envied by the boys. She did so well even while she played basketball almost every night and gallivanted around campus with her friends. Little did they know that she studied arduously when everyone else was relaxing at night. She used to lock herself in her room and read over her notes every day, twice or three times just in case she missed anything. While everyone was studying frantically a few days before the test, she could relax because she had already done it so far in advance. When I am frustrated with school, I ask, "How did you do it, Mom?" She replies the same way every time. "Discipline—that is the key to success. Always make school your first priority. Don't get caught up in your friends when you know you should be studying." I could never force myself to do anything like she could.

And then after all of those countless nights she stayed up studying, after all the years she worked so hard, she had me halfway through her medical school career. I was so unexpected, so taboo that I couldn't stay with my mother for more than a few months. It was a sad day when she handed me over to her mother as she boarded the plane, headed to America, her unknown future gaping at her through the plastic plane window. She left with tears streaming down her soft cheeks and Lakshmi, the goddess of success, at her heels, sent to her by her mother's prayers.

She did extremely well when she got to New York, and she was happy doing her work during the day. It was only at night when her tears started. Through all of the noise at night of the intermittent police sirens and the sound of moving bodies filling up the silence, I swear she could hear me crying across the world. She often had nightmares about me. In one, I was kidnapped by a strange man and sold in the south for a large sum of money and a plot of farmland. In another, her mother forgot to feed me and I starved all alone in my crib. In yet another nightmare, I had been dropped on my head by her careless brother and no one had picked me up.

Aside from these childish fears, however, welled a completely different pool of worry within her. She was scared that I wouldn't want her when I was sent to America, that I would have become so accustomed to my family in India that I wouldn't even know to call her my mother. When she was wrestled awake by the nightmares, the only one that remained after she lay awake and rationalized everything else was her fear of me. Meanwhile, I would lay awake dreaming of how it would feel to be in her feathery embrace.

Now, often at night, she sits in my room and looks at me under my American blanket covered over with an Indian hand-stitched comforter.

"What are you doing, Mom?"

"Nothing, just remembering how you looked when you were younger." I close my eyes again and turn back to her, restless until she slips out of the room quietly, believing that I am actually asleep. As the door creaks open, bringing in shafts of light from the hallway, I can almost hear the faint melody of the song her mother sang to her that night. Every time, I strain my ears to hear her, but I can never quite catch the words.

I doubt that any of us can truly know the feelings of pain and suffering that our ancestors experienced. However, we know that their struggles paved the way for us.

We, as young women of color, have come so far. We have accomplished so much. We have made it through many difficulties and continue to do so each day. Monique's poem reminds us of the struggles we have endured and the ways in which we have overcome them.

MILLENNIUM WOMAN

Monique Beacham, 15
BLACK

From picking cotton and open toes
From sitting in the back of the bus
Riding dirt roads
From being discriminated by the color of my
Skin, that led a new era to begin from marching in corrupt streets
Just for equality.
From good to bad old to new
Wearing polished black shoes from being nobody to somebody
And walking through front doors
From torn old rags to business
Suits and ties
From old fashion to urban
From segregated to overcoming
Racial barriers
I am the Millennium Woman

My biological father did not abandon me. We abandoned him. My mother and I left the big city where we lived with a man who abused my mother and may have done the same to me. I do not at all regret this. My father was a man who was weak inside and took his anger out on the woman he said he loved. I have always been thankful to my mother for leaving when we did. Although I know that my mother and I were the ones who abandoned my father, I cannot help but think that he is the one who truly abandoned me by not behaving as a father should behave. In "Abandoned," Cierra speaks of how her father left her, and how she is angry about his actions and has realized he was not at all the man he should have been. Issues such as these are why I feel a book like this is important—to provide reassurance, comfort, and support. Cierra, I feel you, and I know many other girls do also.

ABANDONED

Cierra Goodloe, 14

BLACK

I don't remember you
not even a kiss or a hug.
No bedtime stories or walks in the park.
When the nightmares came—
    and I called your name
I realized that you wouldn't be there.
The years passed—I got older.
My feelings for you got colder.
Days, weeks, months have passed.
Can't recall when I saw you last.

You weren't there for me
being the man you needed to be.

In my sophomore year of high school I decided I should learn more about me. Therefore, I thought, I should know more about black people. I focused on the obvious ones: Malcolm, Martin, and Rosa.

But I began to want to know about less famous black people. And I wondered why I never learned about them in school. For three years I've tried to get my teachers to teach "black history" (although it is American history). Each year I hear the same thing: "I have to teach this information because it's what will be on the semester test. Maybe you can bring some information in and teach us one of these days."

This is exactly the opposite of what I want. I want to be taught black history because I don't know it. Furthermore, why should the only black student in the class shoulder the responsibility of teaching black history to everyone else?

I want to learn more about myself, just as the European American kids are able to. I want to learn about the influence, the struggle, and the heartache of black people. I have concluded that for now, I will need to learn it on my own. But I hope American children will soon have the opportunity to learn about their own history, wherever their ancestors came from.

"My Heartbeat," by Tiana Phenix (whose pen name is Raw Material), calls out and honors the poets and writers of color who paved the way for us, and who continue to inspire us. I love Tiana's distinctive style.

MY HEARTBEAT

Tiana Phenix, 19
AFRICAN AMERICAN

This is for Gwendolyn who lived a life distilled
For Langston who knew what it felt like to have a dream
For Zora who knew their eyes were watching

To Leroi Jones u gave black more meaning
Than u will ever know
To Donald Goines who wasn't afraid to tell the true tales
    of street hoes
To iceberg slim grandfather of street game Moses of hip-hop
To Claude McKay yardie man of bebop
Who found his way coming home to Brooklyn even when your
    money was tooken?
U spent and bent to write and ignite and take this thing we call
    poetry to flight
U who I spent many a night
To those who heel the fight
Who burn with desire to make simple prose
To those
To those

Who know

To Sonia Sanchez and Fenton Johnson I feel your essence in my
    every note
To Marcus and Move the results of niggaz that vote
To make things simple I could go to my neo-sister Jamaica Kincaid
On some nights my only refuge my only aid
To Alice where I can stand the pain

The oasis the euphoria I feel
To women that make sense of men like Georgia Mcneal
To Ishmael Reed my soul mate indeed
To KRS1, Common, Wordsworth, Mos Def, Rakim,
 Bounty Killah, Buju Banton and
Talib Kweli
In these days of poetic existence we who are so few and far
 in between
U all is all that I need . . .
To make this bitter life sweet
U all are my lifeline the pulse in my heartbeat . . .

Dinner at my house is always hectic. Cooking, trying to get everyone to sit, saying some kind of prayer, and making sure everyone eats are only half of the obstacles of the meal.

However, a new dinner problem has recently occurred: my little sister has begun to demand that she sit with the adults. This creates more obstacles because we cannot deny that she is old enough to sit with us and not spill, but it is also hard because my little brother has not reached that age yet. She is torn between being loyal to her little brother or venturing into the world of adult conversation. She wants very badly to feel accepted by all of us; however, at the age of seven she cannot help but feel a strong (and sometimes stronger) bond with her four-year-old brother.

In "Spades," Hilary describes crossing over to join the adults—in a game of cards. She captures the drama and excitement of a family card game, which to an adult might be ordinary, but to a child is dramatic and filled with great dangers and even greater rewards. Thanks, Hilary, for revealing how a child feels upon entering the world of adults—and in some ways becoming a full-fledged member of the family.

SPADES

Hilary Evans, 13

AFRICAN AMERICAN

I nervously rested my eyes upon the red diamonds and hearts, the black spades and clubs that lay in my sweaty hands. Asking myself if I was up to the challenge that kept on scurrying through my brain like mice. Spades was the name of the game, written into my history as the card game of my family. It was the Christmas of '97 when my family gathered to play this arousing game. Outside the window was the deathly cold winter air of Tennessee without a single flake of ivory snow. The bright orange and yellow flames crackled and danced in the hearth while my grandma Emma, aunt Edna, cousin Emma, and I sat around the kitchen table to play.

"See Edna, I bet that's how she gets her mamma to let her do things," Grandma Emma said annoyingly.

My cheeks flushed crimson as I lowered my head sheepishly, embarrassed about begging to get my way.

"Mm-hm," Aunt Edna replied.

"Well let's get this game started," exclaimed my cousin. That was how it all began. Now the cards were in front of me, and I thought I was ready to play.

The game was under way. I was partnered with my aunt Edna since Grandma Emma and Cousin Emma were partners. It was going terribly. My family was trying to teach me the basics. However, the basics slid through my head like an elusive liquid, not absorbed by my brain. Staring blankly at the shapes and colors on the cards was all I could manage to do. Frantically, my eyes traveled to stare into my partner's. They changed! The warm, brown eyes of my aunt were not there. Instead, there were eyes of evil looking down on me in rage. Obviously, she did not like to lose.

"Hilary, pay attention to what is being played! Hilary, when in doubt, play to win!" Her words were ringing in my ears like the shrill sound of bells. Lost and amazed, I wondered what it was that had taken over my aunt suddenly, in the middle of the game. When my world seemed crashing down by the attack of spades from my aunt, my grandma joined in on the barrage.

"Play right, Hilary," they hissed together. The smile that spread across my face at the beginning of this journey had vanished. I could no longer take the pressure and heat. My eyes blurred with water, and the figures on my cards were unrecognizable. Tears fell slowly down my round, red cheeks.

"See y'all," my aunt Deborah, who had been watching the game the entire time, exclaimed, "you made her cry."

"Don't listen to them, Hilary," my cousin piped in. "They made me cry, too."

"Yeah, Hilary, they are different people when they play cards, like monsters," Aunt Deborah joked. A smile reappeared through my tears and my strength was restored.

We lost, of course, yet I felt like I won personally, not only as a player of Spades, but as a person, too. Tough love was not something I ever really understood, but that day I got a dose of it. I was now able to face and listen to the wrath of family members if I made a mistake in Spades—or in life.

Grandma, you make them, I'll rake them, and we'll go home with the jingle of their quarters in our pockets." My grandma's smile shone through the entire room. It was the Fourth of July and the fan spun overhead, waving cool air above our kitchen table. Aunt Edna, Grandma Emma, Aunt Deborah, my cousin David, and my sister Rachel were all gathered to take part in a traditional family card game of Spades.

I was now an experienced Spades player and I knew my stuff. The cards were dealt and Grandma Emma and I were partners. Our opponents were my two aunts, Edna and Deborah. David was watching us attentively when Aunt Edna suggested that he learn how to play. Thoughts of the past clouded my brain, but I shrugged them off and told myself there was no need to worry. He would be all right. Where Aunt Deborah sat on a chair was now shared with David. Then it was David's turn when he laid out a card.

"Da-Da-Da-David," Aunt Deborah stuttered, "don't you put that card down." A roar of laughter filled the room. My aunt Edna's chuckle was heard over everyone else's. Her body shook with laughter and tears filled her eyes. When I laugh hysterically, no sound comes out. Never have I laughed so hard or so quietly in my life. The roar died down when my sick aunt started coughing.

"Deborah, are you okay? Do you need 911?" my grandma Emma asked seriously. It was that question that ignited the contagious laughter again.

"Shut up, Edna! Somebody get this fool out of here," my grandma pleaded, but this made my aunt Edna shriek with delight. She had her head down and tears of laughter rolled down her cheeks. Everybody else was on the floor with pain in his or her sides from the nonstop banter.

"I'm all right, Mother," was Aunt Deborah's response, which relaxed my grandma's nerves. We played and played and the kitchen was filled with laughter, joy, and love. Grandma and I, of course, won the game. Yet, we did not take my aunts' quarters. Instead, we let them keep them and exchanged winks. Spades, the card game of my family, brings us together for the best of times. It makes us laugh, cry, or both. The game makes us realize how lucky we are to have one another and partake in the joy of family.

PERSON TO PERSON

Because I'm an extrovert, relationships are critical to my well-being. Connecting with people keeps me alive and whole.

As I looked over all of the pieces, I saw many centered on relationships that people had—not just sexual but those with friends and family members. I saw that as we travel through adolescence we are all carefully focusing not only on our own maturity and growth but also on making sure we bond and relate to others.

Person to Person is a place for us to realize who we are when we interact with and relate to others.

Iris, are you sure nothing is going on between you two?"

"Yes, I'm sure, don't you think I would know?"

Rashid's poem had come as a surprise. No one had expected to hear something that serious in the Valentine's Day newsletter. It was just a one-page publication put out by the student council to raise money. Most people had done the usual, given shout outs to friends and made jokes about people. Rashid's, however, was different. He actually wrote a poem, for me.

As I read through all of the pieces I recognized mine—the little, pathetic "secret admirer" joke letter to Rashid. We had agreed to write each other something, and that was all I could think of. Then I skimmed and saw what everyone had been talking about. The poem, although it was only four lines, was beautiful. I immediately thanked him and went on with my day, oblivious to the fact that the poem could actually have been written out of true feelings.

It was not until two days later that I realized what was happening. We were riding from my basketball game having a normal conversation when he just all of a sudden said, "I like you." I was stunned. For some reason I had not previously put the poem and his feelings together, and I was so confused that I did not know what to say. I felt special, liked, and beautiful. Rashid was a great friend and although I knew nothing would happen, I was glad to know his feelings. After that conversation we continued to be friends, and even though we never dated, I am still thankful to him for making me feel so great.

To this day I remember this event fondly. It was not what he did but how he did it. He respected me and did not force himself on me. Instead, he approached me in a kind way and acknowledged my feelings. Thank you, Rashid, for treating me the way I know I deserve to be treated.

In "Chanson d'amour," Shivani tells us a wonderful story of love. Like me, Shivani was treated beautifully, the way she deserved to be. Her story is captivating.

CHANSON D'AMOUR

Shivani Agarwal, 17
INDIAN

The tops of the pine trees just caught the moonlight's gleam on that dark mysterious night. I crept out of the shabby tent and scampered across the wood bridge we built over the gurgling brook. On up past the camping grounds into the blackened woods I went, not knowing exactly where I was going, but reaching a destination nevertheless. I came to "our rock" in a clearing of the dense forest, and there he was, bathed in silver moonlight. As I walked in the dark, a feeling of warmth rushed through my body, and I began to feel a hot sensation behind my eyes.

He sat there calmly, gazing at me with an intensity I had never witnessed before, waiting for me to approach our rock. I thought that night was going to be like any other night. As we lay on the rock, just broad enough for two lovers, we closed our eyes, locked in each other's arms, and naively dreamed of our future together.

A cool breeze came from off the snow-covered mountain before us and swept over our embraced bodies. As the wind swayed back and forth between the silver-soaked leaves of the trees, he started to sing softly. The lilt of his voice lulled me to sleep, and with my eyes closed, I felt the tones of our love come to life and grow.

The words were French and although I didn't know them, I loved their song, the intonations he gave them when he cooed; it became a song that linked two countries, two cultures, two campers, two lovers.

And as we lay there on our rock in the early morning, I thought of the rest of the campers, tucked safely into their flannel sleeping bags, dreaming wonderful dreams, as my dream was becoming real. At that moment, there was no more noise, only our hands delivering the messages of our thoughts and our lips, the trembling heartbeats of our souls. But the music never stopped in our heads; it remained a lulling melody, intensifying our sentiments to their fullest capacities.

We lay there for one more moment, our breath warming each other's faces, our cheeks soaked with tears of gratefulness, the music of his love serenading my heart.

That beautiful tune still seeps into my soul every now and then. I let it come, my body throbbing with love, warm and thrilling. I feel the light behind my clouded eyes and the quivering of my heart. And I just let that smile of knowing creep up into my cheeks, that smile that shows what cannot be sensed or even touched by anything but the music of our love.

Ending any type of relationship is difficult. I remember feelings of loss, anger, and resentment rising when I felt a friendship ending. In "Lately Things," Blair writes of how her relationship is changing. She no longer feels loved, and she misses the way it used to be. I think we can all relate to Blair and feel the pain as she realizes that she and her loved one are no longer as close as they once were.

LATELY THINGS

Blair Revay Bonds, 17
AFRICAN AMERICAN

Lately things aren't the same
You no longer have the
Sparkles in your eyes
You no longer look at
Me as you used to.

You used to tell me
You loved me every day, you
Would hold me in your arms
And say it will be okay.

But now things aren't the same.
Now whenever I come into
View, it seems as though
You always have other
Things to do.
Sometimes I stop and

Ask what's wrong with
You.

And then you just
Look at me and say
Nothin', Boo.

Things are different now,
You no longer see me
As you used to, you
No longer talk
To me as you did before.

I'm starting to feel as
Though I'm just your
Part-time whore. Maybe
Sleeping with you was
A mistake.

At least then your
I love you wouldn't
Sound so fake.

Things are different now.
They're not the same.
Maybe you and I
Have just changed.

Uduak's piece conveys her fierce anger toward her father. As we grow older, it is difficult to break away from our parents—and some of our parents make it nearly impossible to do so by attempting to control us.

While I often feel my parents are too strict, they're not as oppressive as Uduak presents her father. I hope that with Uduak's declaration of independence, she can gain the respect and autonomy she needs.

Untitled

Uduak Onda, 17

BLACK

I try to tell you things, but the words don't pass my clenched teeth. You think my life is a secret. You say I have no emotions, but in reality, everything I'm thinking is written all over my face. You understand me like a sixth-grader understands Shakespeare's work. Instead of asking, you assume. Either you say, "Your appetite has grown, you must be pregnant," or "I never see you studying, your grades have to be dropping." You want me to be your little girl forever, but forever has long gone away. Everything I do is wrong in your perspective, but I'm really just trying to get your attention. You say I'm living my life in a dream, but you're the only one asleep. You clip my wings so I can't fly, but all you do is make my curiosity grow more and more each day. Hiding me from the world won't solve anything. You raised a fine young lady, so learn to trust her. I would and could never do anything to dishonor the family name. You think I don't need your soothing hand. You say if I fall I should bounce right back. When you're out with your friends, you smile and laugh as if you have not one care in the world, but when you're home, your heart turns to coal and your smile turns to a depressed frown. One day you called me to your room; my heart sped up and I felt special. My diary lay open and violated on your bed. When you opened your mouth, the harsh words pierced my ears: "If only you listened to me you wouldn't be in the horrible situation you are in now. I should have realized you would turn out like this. When you were a little girl, I used to look into your eyes and what I saw frightened me. I saw darkness and sorrow. You never seemed to be satisfied. You made people think that I was neglecting you, but in reality, all I was doing was loving you way too much." These words made me weep in my bed for many nights. I lived with you for seventeen years, yet you know a stranger better than you would ever really understand me. What angered me was that you thought you took the time to get to really know me. But if you had, you would have known that I was like a fortune cookie, the best part is in the inside. You hurt me in a spot that no medicine could ever soothe or cure. You even had me thinking, Were all men like you? I try to tell you things, but the words don't pass my clenched teeth. You think my life is a secret. You say I have no emotions, but in reality, everything I'm thinking is written all over my face. You understand me like a sixth-grader understands Shakespeare's work. Instead of asking, you assume. You want me to be your little girl forever, but forever has long gone away.

Hyacinth's parents were divorced when she was two. While she sees her father, there is much she does not share with him. Her poem "Vain Imaginings and Other Artifacts" is a message to him.

VAIN IMAGININGS AND OTHER ARTIFACTS

Hyacinth Wallace-Blake, 14

AFRICAN AMERICAN

While I rested on your chest as a baby
I was unable to see where you'd be
In the future of my feelings
So Grandma's hot chocolate
Holds my hands on "tit-bit-nippley" days,
That even padded bras can't warm
And shirts can't hide
I'm in the women's collard greens and black-eyed peas
Safe on New Year's Eve
Deep within the hefty meal to survive a millennium
When we toasted with fake beer and sipped cider champagne
In Waterford flutes, swinging to the
Rainy Day Rock and Rockafella Skank,
I was gentle when I was young and rocking
But I threw my Ken doll in the furnace
Now I'm surrounded by my kind
These women-folk, penny-collectors and all but blind
Dusting crystal collections of elephant figurines
Trunk up for good luck
I'm told my beauty's only skin deep
To keep me right and righteous
In tight clam diggers and canvas pants,
Stacked and scattered across
A bleach-stained carpeted floor,
I've got my Lemon Pledge and black plume feathers
Gun-metal blue nail polish,
And my mystery bone
The one I found on the street
While running for my life

No one to hold me back
Or on his chest
And rock me rock me just a little while
So I've learned to sing blues solo
And a cappella in the park
Though she still just sings
In the shower and the stairwell
I am from her
The lone songwriter
And I can't stop strumming
Her humming and singing.
Her dreaming, 'til the day she dies
I suck on my Nixie the Pixie pen and contemplate
I score 40s on math quizzes sometimes and
I hid all my baby pictures taken with you
Did you even know I
Wore pink glasses in kindergarten?
So proud and so brave that first day
On the yellow school bus
When the children made me cry
Words still do the same so I've refrained
And never asked you

    Would you even know me, now?

I have had nine best friends in my life: Kelly, Robin, Grace, Emily, Sarah, Alice, Gen, Carrie, and Skyler. With each of them I have shared a little bracelet or ring (the kind on which one says best and the other says friend), which has somehow signified our true feelings for each other. Many of these friendships no longer exist. However, I look at all of them with gratitude. If I hadn't had

Sarah in eighth grade, I don't know what I would have done when I lost my friendship with Emily. If Carrie hadn't welcomed me to my new school, I would have felt like an outcast. And if Grace and Robin hadn't introduced me to the fine world of Saved by the Bell, *I might actually not know about Zach's record of girlfriends or Jesse's stepmom. My best friends have always been there for me when I needed them, and I depend on them a great deal.*

In "Friends," Sarah describes what friendship means to her. She tells of the loss of her best friend, Amber, and how it has been since then. Sarah, your piece is beautiful, and I'm sure you will find another close friend.

FRIENDS

Sarah Richardson, 15

NATIVE AMERICAN / BLACK / WHITE

My best friend, Amber, was there for me through every-thing. All the times I thought I would not be able to pull through, she was there to help me. When I felt I was going insane, she would talk to me, listen to me, and always respect what I said.

Amber and I lived together in a group home for almost two years. We both had problems trusting people, so it was a surprise to us that we became friends so quickly. I trusted Amber with so many things I kept hidden away from everyone else.

When I first met Amber, I called my aunt, so excited, and said, "Auntie, I made a new friend." "No, you didn't, you made a new asso-ciate." My aunt would tell me, "You don't have friends until you are older. You don't even know what a friend is."

Is there a correct definition of a friend? The dictionary describes a friend as someone whom one knows well and is fond of; an intimate associate; a close acquaintance. But you cannot really judge what a friend is based on the dictionary's interpretation. There are people who know each other well and are close, but they are not friends. I think friendship is something that is felt. I believe a friend is someone who fulfills what you need at a time you feel you are lacking something. Since there are no two people who need the same thing, they will not have the same definition of what a friend should be. If you ask me what I want from a friend, it will be different at different times. For example, when I am happy, I want a friend who could be sad but still be glad that I am happy. When I am sad, I want a friend who will comfort me and understand how I feel.

Amber started going through a hard time at our group home. As much as I tried to help, it seemed like she got to a place where I couldn't reach her anymore. Amber started making bad decisions and was discharged from the group home. I will never forget that day.

I have so many things I keep inside that I want to tell someone, but the fear of being judged makes me keep everything locked away. Sometimes the pain of not having many friends hurts so bad that I feel it in my chest. My heart tightens up and I feel a hate rising for everyone, so strongly that my heart flutters up and sort of tickles. I sometimes cradle my hate so that losing Amber won't hurt so badly. I am scared to get close to people because I am still in a lot of pain. I often wonder what she is doing while I am at school and at home. Amber will always be in my heart.

After reading Alicia's poem "Questions and Answers," I felt as though I had missed something. Her voice and words were so powerful and so honest that I knew I wanted to use her poem, but I wanted to understand it better. I e-mailed Alicia, and her response is truly the best introduction to her poem:

When I was younger my father locked my mother, my sister, and me out of our house, and moved my half brother and his mother into our house. Later I found out just how many half brothers and sisters I really have and how close in age we all are. My parents later got married but the topic was never brought up again, and though I forgive him I will never forget.

This poem describes how I felt when everything about my father unfolded and how I could never look at him the same way again.

QUESTIONS AND ANSWERS

Alicia Carrington, 16
AFRICAN/CARIBBEAN

So I should be just like you?
One who had 4 women and 8 kids too?
One who never had a steady bed?
Who loves to make sweat run down young girls' legs
Stealing their youth and bringing youth on to them
Make up your mind, who do you want to be with then?
The time you locked me out was probably the answer
You changed the lock,
I rang the bell, you didn't answer.
You wouldn't look back and didn't even care
Just as long as those inside are happy, huh?
Why won't you answer my question
Because you don't know why?
You got no good answers?
You got no good replies?
When you came back in my life
I didn't know what to do
You never asked me any questions
But in that way I'm just like you

If you asked me I couldn't tell you
And I don't know why
Because I too ain't got no good answers
And I got no good replies

My mother has always supported me, loved me, and been there for me. When I was eleven years old she married, and I realized I was no longer number one in her life. I had to make way for not only a new husband but also a new baby.

I did not hate my little sister for the attention she received, or my stepfather, but instead myself. I got angry with myself for not taking advantage of the time I'd had before. She still loved me, but she had other priorities. She had to take care of her new baby and her husband. Instead of worrying about me constantly, she made sure she treated us all equally.

As I've grown older I've come to understand my mistake and to realize that it wasn't my fault. I know I should have taken more time with her, but I also know I can't erase the past. While my mother may not have always provided the large quantity of hugs I wanted, I love her with all my heart. I will never get those years back, but I will always cherish all the years I have had with her.

In her poem "Her Dance," Jennifer writes of how she feels about her father's new relationship. She realizes her mistakes of taking things for granted, but she also feels the pain of what it's like to no longer be number one.

HER DANCE

Jennifer Oda, 17
JAPANESE/BRAZILIAN

Children always take things for granted
Think things will always be there
I pushed you away
God, I'm stupid.

When she arrived, I hated it
Despised her
Warm images of you and her
Irritate me
Torment
Aching
She is better than I

Heavy teardrops stain my shirt's thirsty sleeve
My room lit solely by peeking slices of yellow light
Slanting through cracks in the doorway
Solitude sitting next to me on the floor

She took you away
I can't forgive her
Your voice on the phone is distant
I picture your body slouched in the chair
Hand dangling to the side, phone pressed against your
   deafened ear
Staring at her
I
Need you

You don't hear me

Your loving lips no longer smile for me
Our dance is hers now

Longing for so many years to confess
How much I have always loved you—
More than myself

It's too late
You're no longer in my grasp.

*I*n this piece, Jessica expresses her fear of opening herself up to love—and to the potential for getting hurt. I relate to "I Put on a Mask" because I can say that I have only really opened up completely to a few people, and even then I found it difficult.

In part, I know this feeling is one reason I wanted to create this book—so that I as a girl of color can learn to depend on other women of color. I no longer want to feel alone or feel as though I need to bottle up my emotions. I no longer want to feel that if I open myself up to another person, I will be hurt.

I hope someday Jessica will be able to take off her mask. Even if she feels unsafe in a relationship, I hope she will be able to count on her sisters of color. Maybe someday Jessica will be able to call me, and let me in that door, so that we can be there for each other.

I Put on a Mask

Jessica L. Farley, 18
AFRICAN AMERICAN

I want to love you.

I want to give you as much of myself as I possibly could. I want to shower you with kisses and listen to your voice. I want to wrap my arms around you and feel secure, loved, protected, admired. . . .

But I just can't do it.

Some may ask why not, and so I ask myself—why not? Why don't I have the right to love? Or feel loved?

Though those questions cloud my head, I seem to know the answer so very well. Yet, it is one I wish I did not.

It is because of fear.

Fear is holding me back and not letting me love you or get close to you in the way I want.

I am afraid.

I am afraid that if I give you my heart, you will stomp on it. I am afraid that if I give you my innocence, you will turn it into guilt. I am afraid that if I show you laughter, you will bring me tears. I am afraid that if I let you inside, you will break me and not stick around to fix it.

And, because of this, I close the door to love.

I close the door to you.

I put on a mask, not only to hide my face, but also my heart. To keep me from being hurt when you decide to betray me or walk away. To not let you get to me and put a dent in my heart that could never be fixed.

I live in my insecurities because I frown at the person who loses the chance to love, but still I realize, I am frowning at myself.

Tayo's poem depicts a routine she had fallen into with her sex partner—a routine of secrecy that became damaging to Tayo's sense of self. Her style in "The Routine" conveys her anger over being used sexually. I applaud Tayo on her ability to break loose, and I hope that others out there who are in routines similar to Tayo's learn to get out and stay out.

THE ROUTINE

Tayo Darrell, 17
AFRICAN AMERICAN

It starts with a call
Not a planned call
A call from out of the blue
Whatever day of the week, whatever time
He doesn't call me when I beep him
He calls when he pleases
"Hi, what's up, how are you?"
Telling me the same thing he told me last time
Just get to the point
You want to see me
WHEN
Tomorrow, the next day or the next
WHEN
In the morning
Then in the morning I go up there
SNEAK
Into the apartment as if you are illegal
SHHH
Because no one can hear you

HIDE
Because no one can see you
PEEK
Out first if you want to use the bathroom
COVER
Your mouth when you want to laugh loudly
Talk, Talk, Talk
Watch TV
Sex, then silence
Talk, Talk, Talk
Sex again
Silence again
It's over for the day
LEAVE
But wait before you leave
LISTEN
To hear if anybody's in the hallway
WAIT
A while then leave
When it first began
I used to receive a call after I saw him
NOT ANYMORE
Then the next day
Or a couple of days after that
I'll see his girlfriend come over
Him and her
Walking hand in hand
Knowing that she has no routine
He calls her when she wants him to
She comes over and spends days there if she pleases
She doesn't have to sneak as if she is illegal
She can laugh as loudly as she wants
Because it doesn't matter if anybody hears her
She isn't hidden

She isn't his secret
Am I not good enough why I must go through
THE ROUTINE
Then she leaves
And the ROUTINE
Happens all over again
It's been happening for over a year
NOT ANYMORE
I'm no longer his toy that he throws away
And picks up when he pleases
I'm free.

When I received Alicia's piece there was a note from her mother attached. The note explained that Alicia had never before expressed her feelings on paper about her mother's diagnoses of breast cancer. Alicia's mother also wrote how happy she was to see her daughter speak out on this issue. I included the piece in this chapter because of the loving and powerful relationship Alicia describes between herself and her mother.

UNTITLED

Alicia Lea Haley, 17
AFRICAN AMERICAN

When my mother was first diagnosed with breast cancer I was thirteen years old. At the time I knew nothing about this illness or what it could do to you. All that I knew was that my mom was really sick and she had to be in the hospital for a while. I felt confused, lost, and scared. When my mom came home from the hospital, she looked really tired and weak, but she kept saying that she was okay. I knew she wasn't all right; I could see it in her eyes.

One night around midnight I heard a strange noise. When I got up to see, I found my mom in the bathroom, looking in the mirror and crying. All of her hair had come out. I began to cry because I felt that my mom didn't deserve this, she didn't do anything to anybody.

By the time her chemotherapy treatment was over her hair had grown back and she had one breast. It was pretty funny when I first saw it; she looked like a girl on one side and a boy on the other. We made the best out of the situation.

Years passed, and everything was going well until the night that my mom said she wanted to tell me something. From the look on her face I knew something was wrong. She told me to sit down and not to get scared because it wasn't anything serious. My oldest brother, Aaron, was there, too. I had thought that I would never in my life hear those words, but I was wrong. She said, "I have breast cancer again." The minute she said it I began to cry. I felt like I couldn't take it anymore, I couldn't stand to see my mom suffer and still be so strong.

But this time I knew more about the illness, so this time I wouldn't let it get the best of me. I was like her nurse. I would bathe her and fix her soup. It was pretty fun being her nurse—she was a lousy tipper, but I loved her for that anyway. Well, once again, months passed and everything was back to normal.

Now it has been five years that my mother has been a breast cancer survivor. We all salute her for staying strong and keeping the faith through all the chaos. My mom and I have a relationship like no other. I can tell her everything and she can tell me everything. She's my best friend. The only thing I am afraid of is this illness; she means the world to me, and if anything were to happen to her I would die.

This taught me a lesson: to spend more time with my mom, because life is short. You should spend your life with someone you love. Mom, I love you and I will always love you, no matter what. Even if I can say my breasts are bigger than my mom's.

Girls of color have forever been caretakers. This is what we are taught, from baby-sitting our siblings to cooking for our families. Part of being a caretaker means defending men of color—our fathers, uncles, brothers, and, someday, our sons. We have been trained to stand by them, to protect them from harm, and most of all fight whatever battles they may need help fighting.

Because people of color have had to stick by one another just to survive, very little has been done to help women of color claim their own rights. We were busy fighting for civil rights when the feminist movement passed us by, and we've been torn between being black, Latina, Native American, and Asian on one hand, and being women on the other hand.

We as females of color have been told that sexism does not exist for us or is not important. Yet it runs rampant throughout our communities. I cannot even begin to count all the disrespectful and derogatory things I have heard come out of the mouths of men of color. I feel guilty for thinking this is wrong. I feel guilty for outwardly accusing men of color of such treatment. I know there are many wonderful, respectful men of color, so I have no reason to be angry. Yet still I am.

I believe women of color have every right to hold our men accountable for their behavior toward us. We are beautiful, strong women and deserve to be treated as such. In fact, our men should be outraged; they should be furious about our treatment and do whatever they can to change it immediately. They should not tolerate having their mothers, sisters, and daughters subjected to such oppression.

However, we need to be enraged, too. We need to stop making excuses for our men. We need to work together, to become a force together, fighting for equality for men and women of all colors.

In "Battered Butterfly," Kristla speaks of her treatment by a man in her life. It sickens me to know that anyone suffers from such abuse. I hope that Kristla continues to grow and learns to trust again. Perhaps someday men and women of color can strive for equality, together.

BATTERED BUTTERFLY: A STORY OF AN ABUSIVE RELATIONSHIP

Kristla Wingo, 17
AFRICAN AMERICAN

I don't even remember when I fell in love with him. It's like a page missing from a book. I totally don't remember. Maybe he beat it out of me. I don't know. It just happened. I didn't have a clue why he picked me. I mean, every girl in the neighborhood wanted him. They were all certainly much better looking than I was. For the strangest of reasons, he chose me. Everyone who knew me said I was extremely lucky to have him in my life. I certainly felt lucky. He made me feel so good on the inside. Romeo was what everyone called him. He was truly a Romeo. So charming and outgoing. A pure sweetheart. Handsome, too. Very attractive, noticeably popular. Everything I thought I was looking for.

Those characteristics soon faded away. It then seemed as if he'd never been that way. Things began to take a dramatic turn. For no reason at all, he'd just get really angry and lash out at me. Sometimes he wouldn't hit me. He might just shake me or push me. I would let it slide. Other times, he'd hit me so hard across the face with his hands. It hurt like hell, too. He'd punch me and choke me, even slam me on the floor. I'd cry. I'd cry so much it would entice him to say he was sorry. Sometimes he wouldn't say he was sorry. He'd just leave me crying on the floor of his living room. Every day, I'd go home to my father all bruised and beat up. He'd always ask me what happened. I'd say an accident in gym or a locker hit me in the face. But a locker accident can't happen every day. One day, my father invited Romeo over to dinner. He accepted the invitation. God, it was such a front. He made it seem like our relationship was perfect and like I was the light of his life in front of my family. That was the last time I ever saw him smile at me . . . ever.

After the dinner at my house, I thought it was going to get better. Well, it didn't. It got so bad that he actually started beating me up in school. He got suspended once because he punched me in the mouth for asking him a question. Soon, he would see me talking to other guys who were only friends, and just slam me up against the locker. He'd scream in my face, asking me what business I had talking to the guy. When I'd try to tell him the guy was just my friend, he'd slap the taste out of my mouth. I'd cry. He always would embarrass me in school and in public. Once he grabbed me from out of nowhere while I was on my way home and slammed me against a brick wall, choking me nearly to death. Tears were welling up in my eyes. All because his nosy-ass friend told him that I was talking to this guy in the school courtyard. I couldn't even breathe. Fighting was useless. He was so much bigger than I was. His grip was tightening around my throat. I was crying hysterically while he screamed in my ear. All I could say was *I'm sorry*. I couldn't stop crying. I was already scream-ing, telling him to let me go. A voice from far away yelled at him and told him to let me go. He did, but not before he slapped me deaf. He actually hit me so hard, I couldn't hear. My legs trembled as I stood. My whole body grew numb. I couldn't feel anything as I gasped for air. My brain was saying "RUN," but my body shook with a confused fear. The man who said he loved me had just choked the shit out of me. My face stung from the blow to my cheek. My head ached from the repeated slams against the hard wall. The first thing I did was walk away. Fast. He didn't follow me; he just called my name repeat-edly, in an apologetic fashion. I didn't bother to turn around; I kept on walking until I got home. Behind my front door, against the wall, there was a mirror. I shut the door to look in the mirror. In the future, I would spend many days in front of that mirror, tending to my black eyes and busted lips. I stayed with him because I thought things would get better. I thought he'd look at me again with that guilt in his eyes, and he'd love and want me again.

I didn't learn my lesson until one weekend. I was out with my friends at a party. Things went smoothly for about two hours, until Romeo showed up with his crew. And it just so happened that I was dancing with a couple of my friends in a little semicircle. He saw me and almost lost his mind. I didn't see him coming, but I felt his hand wrap around my hair. He pulled me by my hair toward the entrance. I was fighting and kicking. My friends leaped on him, fighting him off. I was glad they were helping me, but it was useless. He had a firm grip on my hair, and my kicking didn't help because he picked me up and carried my screaming body out of the party hall. When we were outside, he put me down, letting me stand up straight. I thought that was the end and that he wasn't going to hit me. Well, once again I underestimated him. When his punch hit me, my head hit the hard concrete ground. I just lay there with tears burning my cheek. On the other side of my face, there was a wound from scraping my face against the ground. I couldn't even get up. My torso ached badly from the hit. He stood in front of me, yelling, "Get UP!" I couldn't stand. I started to crawl back toward the door of the hall, but he didn't let me go that far. He picked me up and immediately began to choke me. I begged him to stop, and I even told him I was sorry for whatever I had done. He said, "You can't apologize for being a whore. That's what you are!" I was really crying now. He wouldn't let me go. I finally raised my hand and dug my nails into his face. By reflex, he let me go to grab his face. I took off running toward my house. I lived eight blocks away. I ran, but passed out when I was a block away. When I awoke, I was in the living room on the sofa. My dad and my sister were there. My father knew what had happened to me. He said, "He'll never set foot in this house." And within a week, Romeo was behind bars for possession of marijuana.

After I recovered from the beatings, I began seeing a psychiatrist for counseling and treatment of depression. I was depressed because I wasn't with him. I didn't know how to handle the fact that I was alone and no one was beating me up anymore. I never talked to Romeo again. After six months in counseling I finally regained my self-worth and pride. I had to work on learning to trust other men. I didn't date too much after that. I felt that the comfort of my friends was all I needed. I'm now a junior in high school with six months of terror behind me. Taking one day at a time. Maybe one day, I will learn to trust again. I don't know. I'm just happy to be alive.

The whistle blew.

We all lined up as usual and began the trek to our classrooms after our exhausting recess. Alex came up to the line late and demanded that I let him stand in front of me so he wouldn't get in trouble. Without even waiting for a response from me, he quickly added, "I wish segregation never ended. That way I wouldn't have to go to school with you." I was stunned by his comment. I wanted to turn and tell someone, but no one would understand. No one looked like me.

As we went up to the coatroom, I could no longer hold it in. I burst into tears and was soon surrounded by the seven other girls in my class. They demanded to know what had happened and though not one of them could relate, they all tried to comfort me and make me feel better. After I calmed down I realized how I would look. I didn't want Alex and the rest of the boys to know I had been crying, so I went with the other girls into the bathroom. Together they helped me clear up the red blotches on my cheeks and they splashed water on their own to act as if they had been crying. We laughed at what fools we looked like and I soon perked up. Finally we went into the classroom and I felt better.

In retrospect I believe I was not upset over the comment from Alex as much as I was by not wanting to deal with it. I was in third grade and had no comprehension of what or how I was supposed to feel. And although the girls in my class also didn't understand how I felt, they knew I was crying and they offered the support they could give. Those girls had created a safe place for me. We had bonded in that bathroom, and although we could not erase the color line that so obviously separated us, we came together for that moment. And even though I would handle such a situation differently today, that was exactly the support I needed at the time. From that incident I learned that although race is always an important factor, it is okay to leave it on the sidelines and offer support to others.

Itoro's story is very much like my own. Claudia was her support system and no matter what color they both were, Itoro needed her. Itoro's piece shows the importance not only of friendship but also of the ability to overcome adversity and succeed.

A WELCOMED IDENTITY

Itoro Akpan, 17

AFRICAN AMERICAN

"Itoro?"

"What?" I replied, sharply reversing my attention from my biology paper to the cracking voice underneath me.

"Are you trying out tonight for the team?" whispered the mud-color-eyed, blond girl squinched under my lab table.

"Claudia!" exclaimed the professor from across the room.

Claudia sighed and lifted her short and frail body. Seated, she turned and smiled to me.

Claudia Hart was the only white student who was friends with me while I attended my eighth-grade year at Trickum Middle School. Since my first day, she had created a calm atmosphere for me at my first all-white school. She knew I was an outstanding gymnast who was scared to perform in front of the school because of my color. Claudia persuaded me to be the first African American to join that year's Trickum Tigers Gymnastics Team.

As I quickly slipped into my blue leotard in the locker room, a redheaded girl vigorously pushed against my shoulder. I turned and noticed Crystal McKillian, the most popular girl in school. Haughtily, she stared at me and asked, "You're trying out tonight?"

"Yeah."

She hissed and threw her hands on her hips. "If I were you," she added, "I wouldn't."

"Why?" I asked.

She giggled distinctly and whispered, "Nigger."

Alone, I stood there in astonishment as she trotted away. She called me a nigger. Why? I could only reflect in silence and shudder from anticipation and fear.

When all twelve gymnasts entered the gym, a thunder of applause vibrated. Nervously, I glanced through the audience to see if I could find Claudia.

I was called to perform on the balance beam. I rose and smiled toward the audience, and in return they gave me no response. Their white faces watched me as I marched toward the beam. I climbed onto it and started to dance my way down to the opposite end. I managed to bend backward, grab hold of the beam, and swing my body over. After landing, cheers came from around the gym. I smiled and finished the routine with a perfect dismount.

After several performances, Crystal was ahead of me by a few points. I waited meekly for my last performance on the floor exercise. As I approached the floor, the audience cheered. I tapped my foot to the first beats of "YMCA" and performed a series of somersaults diagonally across the floor. I pranced my way to the end of my routine and added strong tumbling techniques.

I was shocked when my scores beamed from the scoreboard— two points above Crystal's. I was awarded and congratulated by everyone in the gym. Lastly, Claudia and I embraced, both sharing our happy moment in tears.

Without Claudia's loyal guidance, I would have never shared my athletic talents with the school. Because of our friendship, I have a healthier identity and personality. I have achieved not only a sense of racial equality, but also joyful memories of my last years at Trickum Middle School.

All I can really say about Tiana's stunning poem is that I want this feeling. I want to know what it is like to have no control over my emotions and fall in love with someone because "it's fresh and new." I want true love.

UNTITLED

Tiana Phenix, 19
AFRICAN AMERICAN

it's like
u came and it's like
i see me
in u and
fear is obsolete
over paths and distances
he and i from same origin
and it's like
in every mirror in my sleep

i felt like i made the dream
and i followed thru on that divine blueprint
finally
with no new expectations
and it's green
cuz it's fresh and new
and especially touched in some unfamiliar way
i coulda been easy
so easy so easy
i hope he sees me
in his trumpet
and in everything in relation to
now in the now i drowned
and submerged in beautiful cosmic seas
i his moon and him my sun make a catch and chase
made me smile from the inside out
inspired to complex prose and way of expression
with no discretion
in smoky bliss
and great epiphany we emerge
i won't walk away
first there was darkness
and god created light and saw that
it was good
and he came
with message unknown
and excess unwillingly willingly shed and inspiration
in twists and turns of blue and red and vibrant colors
camouflaged by laughter and smiles
and it is and exists in a natural state of
something i refused to define as anything other than what it is
it is illumination and freshness and
no exact rest or ending and hazy

beginning
and majestic happening
incited me to
to do what could be . . .

Maribel's piece was submitted in Spanish and in English, and the two versions follow here. I love this poem and the fact that she sent it in two languages. The way Maribel describes love allows all of us who have been in love as well as those who have yet to experience it to understand the beautiful feeling it creates. Thanks, Maribel, for the exquisite poem and for sharing your culture with your translation.

UNA ROSA EN MI JARDIN

Maribel Lopez Guzman, 17
MEXICAN AMERICAN

Pequena y tierna
Como un boton de rosa
Dentro de un gran jardin
Abriendo dia tras dia

Tomando un hermoso color
Y nuevas dimensiones

Sin duda alguna
Siendo de entre todas

Una de las mas bellas
Una de las puras
Y una de las de mejor aroma.

Radiante y esplendorosa
Como el sol en una tarde de verano;
Capaz de coger en su regazo a todo aquellos
Q'necesitan de tu calor
En esos dias tan frios
Y a todos aquellos
Q'necesitan de tu luz tu calor
En esos dias de obscuridad

Tu, pequena rosa
Radiante sol,
Decora mi vida
Ilumina mi alma.

Tu, q'desde q'brtaste
Has setado decorando
Todo mi jardin

Tu, q'desde cuando te vi
Por primera vez me llenaste de paz.

Tu q'a pesar de ser aun
Un pequeno capullo
Eres mejor q'una gran flor.
Tu, q'cruzaste mi camino,
Trayendole color, aroma y forma
Quedate conmigo y nunca
Sola me dejes.

A ROSE IN MY GARDEN

Tiny and tender
Like an unblossomed rose
Within a large garden
Opening day after day.

Forming a beautiful color
And new dimensions.

Without a doubt,
Being among all,
One of the most beautiful,
One of the most pure
And one of the most sweet aromas.

Radiant and splendorous
Like the sun
In a summer afternoon
Capable of collecting in her embrace
All of them that need your warmth
In those cold days,
And all of them that need
Your light and color
On those dark days.

You, tiny rose,
Radiant sun,
Decorate my life,
Illuminate my soul.

You, since I saw you
for the first time
have filled me with peace.

You, even after being
a small rosebud
are greater than a grand flower.

You, that crossed my path
Bringing it color, aroma and form
stay with me and never let me
be alone anymore.

OURSELVES INSIDE AND OUT

Ourselves Inside and Out is about identity. As teenagers, we are in the process of developing our selves, of discovering and embracing what makes each of us unique. As females, we are working to find a strong identity and direction in a society that objectifies and sexualizes women, especially young women. And, as people of color, we are challenged to develop a positive identity in a deeply racist nation.

In this section, girls have written on topics from spirituality to sex to school, exploring their many identities and the possibilities they envision for themselves and their future.

When I was younger I always wanted to be a skater. Not because I really enjoyed watching or learning how to skate, but instead because I wanted to impress the guys. I wanted to show them that I knew how to skate, that I was talented, and that I was worthy of their respect. I never really learned because I lacked one key element (besides skill): motivation. Shimere, unlike myself, has accomplished her goal of becoming a skater. She has motivation and drive, and she definitely has my respect.

I Am a Female Skater

Shimere Etheridge, 14
AFRICAN AMERICAN

I am sore, I am weak
From all this sweat I really reek
A girl on the half pipe?
Get real, they say
But who cares what they think?
I'll have it my way
Every weekend I go and get better than the last
True, I bust a lot
And afterwards I don't look so hot
But that's okay, people say
'Cause I got something other girls don't got
Courage to get up there
And try my very best
At least I am trying
And that gets their respect
Yeah, I'm a girl, a girl who skates
I got bruises to prove it
And lots of aches
But for now I am trying my very best
I hope you can see that
And give me some respect

When I was a child, I had the opportunity to play Capture the Flag with kids in my neighborhood. I remember it clearly. Emily and I would try to gather as

many people as possible to play, and as the game went on more kids would peek out of their houses and join in.

Troy was always the general. He would have a walkie-talkie (no one had another one, so he talked to himself), a periscope so if we all of a sudden were covered by water he could see what was coming, and a full-body uniform. When the night officially ended, Troy would always give our team a pep talk on what we did well and how we could have improved. I remember standing and giggling with Emily, but making sure Troy didn't see.

Throughout the evening all of us would have experienced numerous fights, a lot of laughter, and wonderful memories to enjoy when we were older.

"Horizontal Ups and Downs" by Shawntai was one of the pieces I connected with the most. Not because it was about racism, or the struggle of being a girl of color, but instead it captured what I remember and cherish the most: my childhood. "The Child of Our Younger Years" by Neftara was also a piece I strongly identified with. So often I try to make sure I hold on to my childhood, but then I realize that it is always a part of me. The way in which Shawntai and Neftara describe the details of childhood made me feel the joys, wonders, discoveries, and freedom of childhood all over again.

HORIZONTAL UPS AND DOWNS

Shawntai Genell Brown, 15

AFRICAN AMERICAN

I am eight years old and I am the princess of Mansfield. "Mom, can I go to Brittany and Brandon's house?" I ask. She says yes. I stuff my locket in my shirt so that no one will ask to wear it, put on my purple sunglasses that turn pink in the sun, and walk out the door. I stroll down the sidewalk and see Brittany, Brandon, and K. J. already playing. The boy whose name I don't know and don't want to know so I never ask is also there. They are walking toward me with fluffy blankets, colorful plastic tiaras, crowns, sticks, leaves, and juicy grass.

"The princess is coming!" they yell. "Prepare the royal stuff!" They reach me and tie the purple blanket stained with dirt around my neck as a royal cape. Brandon places the tiara with sparkling jewels on my head and hands me a stick that is long and lumpy like burnt oatmeal as my royal scepter.

"I want to play," Tiffany yells, stepping outside, followed by her younger sister Jennifer. I normally would have stopped by to get them since they live next door to me, but I am mad at Tiffany for something I can't remember. "Why is she always the princess?" Tiffany asks with a stuck-up face and an attitude lurking in her throat. I am beginning to remember why I am mad at her. I was the princess every day we played because I am the oldest, besides the boy whose name I don't know, and K.J. says it is because I am the prettiest, even though it makes me sick to look at him every time he says it.

"We have to have a prince," Brittany says. Brandon was the prince last week. Every time the boy whose name I don't know is the prince, I refuse to play. K.J. is volunteering like he does every time, grinning and blowing kisses at me. He is chosen and smiles hard as if his cheeks are going to explode. Jennifer, Brittany, and Tiffany help K.J. put on his royal attire. He finally is dressed and he hugs me saying, "Kiss me, Princess," and I scream in disgust, and he lets me go, looking as if he is going to cry like last time. The boy whose name I don't know prepares the royal meal out of grass and leaves. K.J. and I pretend to eat the food as our royal servants entertain us with dancing. K.J. tries to hold my hand and I let him because he has been nice to me for the last fifteen minutes. We play and act and pretend as streetlights come on along with curfew and reading time at my house. The boy whose name I don't know gives me a flower and I like him. Even though the game is over he becomes the prince for a moment. He says his name but I do not hear him because I am walking home so he won't see me smile. I smile hard like K.J.'s exploding cheeks, but the cute boy whose name I don't know doesn't see me, and no one has asked to borrow my locket, and for a moment I feel like a real princess.

THE CHILD OF OUR YOUNGER YEARS

Neftara O. Clark, 18
BLACK

Do we ever lose the wonder years that made up our childhood?
Do the memories of playing jump rope with the neighborhood kids
Ever truly go away?
Does the feeling of unquestionable innocence drain from our
    physical cells and mind,
Once we enter into the mysterious, yet unique world of adulthood?
Do we ever forget the long days spent on Grandma's porch hop-
    ing and daydreaming?
Do we ever again get to taste and actually savor the flavors of our
    virginity and purity once it has been traded in for a few
    moments of what we think is uncontrollable passion?
Does the fear-free gleam that existed in our young eyes still
    reflect such light in our older ones?
Do we allow the memories of those carefree feelings of running
    through the mud after a big rainstorm to cause giggles to
    escape our fully developed lips when the thought comes up?
Do peanut butter and jelly sandwiches still taste the same
    properly
Cut in twos as they tasted mushed and spread across our faces as
    children?
Do we maintain our sense of joy for every second of every
    minute of every day,

Just playing with our toys, once we are given the constraints of 8
to 5 workdays?
Do we ever forget the sweet smells that engulf our childhood
imaginary gardens and fantasy worlds?
Once we choose to take on mature responsibilities and activities?
Does the laughter and humor of our younger years get to sustain
an existence or a space within the folds of our disciplined lives?
Do we get to remember the feelings of pure happiness and content-
ment we experienced from just sitting and playing in the dirt?
Does one get to imagine the lands of princesses and princes once
they have closed themselves off to the third eye of the mind?
Do adults truly lose their inner child, their younger souls and
spirits to the clutches of the world today?
Oh how I sit and wonder only if we allow it to be forgotten, shall
it be,
For our souls today remain our souls of yesteryears.

*A friend of mine jokes that she can be independent, as long as someone is with
her. She and I are a lot alike. I have always thought of myself as being able to
do and accomplish things on my own, yet I also depend on people a great deal.
However, by depending on people I am not in any way decreasing my individu-
alism and independence. In order for me to stay healthy, I need people in my
life whom I am able to depend on emotionally, people whom I can talk to
about anything, and people who will give me the support I need when I need
it. I am independent in action and feeling, yet I rely on people to be there for
me—and am proud of it.*

*In "Do the Feminist Thing," Meredith speaks of her own battles with
allowing people to help her. Her experience with letting people in is common among many women of color. So often we seem to keep people out as*

a defense mechanism; we may offer to help them, but we don't allow them to help us. We can all learn from Meredith——that it's not weak to need or ask for help.

DO THE FEMINIST THING

Meredith King, 19

AFRICAN AMERICAN

So I'm sitting in this white lady's office and she's telling me that she thinks I need to see a psychologist or therapist or something. She's like, "What are you feeling? What are you thinking? I want to KNOW you. Let me in," and I'm sitting across from her thinking, What the hell is going on? But maybe I should back up.

First, this white lady is my boss; her name is Karen. I work at a Women's Community Center, where I was designing an event for women of color activists on my college campus. That's basically my job as a black woman at a predominantly white center——to diversify. But she calls me into her office, Karen does, and she tells me very nicely, "Maybe this event is not for you . . . I'm not sure you're capable of handling it." I am stunned by what she is saying to me. It doesn't make sense and it feels like it is coming out of nowhere. My heart is broken, and I try to hold back the tears that begin to brim in my eyes. There is a knot in my throat and I am afraid to speak. She continues, "I think you need to see a psychologist. I feel like, this whole year you've been trying to tell me something. You've been trying to tell me that you are depressed and need help." At this point, holding back my tears becomes a merely futile effort, and they start streaming down my face. I look her straight in the eye, with as much defiance as I can muster, challenging her to hurt me more than she already has.

SHE sits in a room, looking out the window to the world outside. SHE wonders how people can live such carefree lives outside the room. Out the window SHE sees bodies, hears voices, but not people. The voices are disjointed from the bodies, and the words don't make sense. Not to her ears. SHE hears birds chirping, squirrels scurrying, and SHE wonders what her life would be like on the outside. SHE wonders how the hell SHE's going to get out of the room.

I stop listening to the words coming from her mouth. I've heard them all before. And after a while they all start to sound the same anyway. I start listening to the conversation of the people on the other side of the door.

"So are your parents coming for graduation?"

"Yeah, but it'll be kind of weird for them to meet Dan."

The voices outside start to mingle with the bullshit flowing steadily from Karen's mouth. "When you cried at the staff training a couple of weeks ago . . ."

"Dan is such a great guy, I'm sure they'll . . ."

"And then when you told me about your friend's suicide attempt . . ."

"Yeah, we've been together for about five, no, six months. God, he would kill me if he thought I didn't know how long we'd been together . . ."

"And then the cutting . . ."

"You two are so cute together. What are you going to do after graduation . . ."

"I'm willing to get you some good help. Even off campus. I will take you if necessary. But you need to see someone . . ."

"We should have a big party . . ."

"Do the feminist thing and help yourself . . ."

I realize that this fucked-up, one-sided conversation will continue as long as I let it. I cut off Karen's ramblings right as I envision myself grabbing her by the shoulders and shaking her until she understands what she has done. "Are we finished?" I ask bluntly.

"We're done whenever you say the word."

I get up to leave, but she obviously doesn't mean what she says. She calls me back. "Don't leave like that," she says.

"I thought we were done," I say.

"Can I at least have a hug?"

I pause at the realization that this woman just took a bite out of my heart and wants me to hug her for it. I take a step toward her, and she covers the rest of the distance and quickly throws her arms around me. She holds me tight and strokes my hair as if I were her child and she wanted to protect and nurture me. My arms hang loose, bound to my sides by her embrace. I let her hug me and don't even have to convince myself to feel numb. I am numb. She squeezes me tighter, wanting me to return her embrace so that she can go home and tell herself that it's okay. That she did the right thing.

I don't give her the satisfaction.

She goes home and tells herself that she did the right thing anyway.

Sometimes SHE has flashbacks of things that happened in the past. Well, not exactly flashbacks. But sometimes SHE gets so caught up in a memory that SHE forgets about the present.

I lock the door to my dorm room, close the shades, keep the lights off, crawl into my bed, and push my face into my pillow as sobs rack my body. In my head I can hear Karen's words over and over again. "I want to know what you're thinking . . . feeling . . . Do the feminist thing . . . help yourself . . ." I'm back there, in her office again, afraid to speak and afraid to leave. Her words haunt my thoughts and mingle with all the things I should have said. "I'm fine . . . I don't need any help . . . mind your own business . . . Black people don't see psychologists . . . why are you doing this to me . . ."

SHE believes that SHE is back there, living in her memory. SHE reenacts every aspect of the moment, playing the roles of all the people involved. SHE remembers what SHE said, and should have said, what SHE thought, and should have thought, what SHE felt, and should have felt, looking at the ordinary passerby as another crazy person talking to themselves. Sometimes the recollection is so deep that SHE needs something powerful to jerk her back into the present day. SHE reaches into her drawer and fishes around for a second until her hand closes on what SHE is looking for. SHE pulls it out and feels the cold sharpness against her forearm. Just the feel of the razor blade against her arm makes her sigh with comfort and remembrance. SHE rips the blade across her arm three times and breathes a sigh of relief. There is a little pain, but it is a welcome pain. SHE knows this pain and embraces it each time it visits. It brings her back to the present, back to life, and makes everything okay again. Mostly there is just cold, like catching a draft up a short skirt. SHE lets the blood drip onto her bedcovers, not bothering to bandage her arm. SHE falls back onto her bed and lays there in satisfied silence.

I spend almost three whole days like this. I pretend the incessant knocking on my door doesn't exist, and when it stops, I leave the darkness of my room only to use the bathroom. I keep asking myself how someone I trusted as a friend and mentor could hurt me like this. The knocking on my door returns, and becomes heavier and more urgent. *SHE doesn't need help* . . . I don't need help . . . I don't need help . . . *SHE needs help* . . . I . . . need . . . help . . .

The inevitable realization comes just as my door flies open and concerned friends and a Resident Assistant with a master key come spilling into my room, hugging me, shaking me, questioning me. I can't respond to them. There's too much going on inside me. Too many things it hurts to face.

I realize that my anger at what Karen said to me kept me from admitting to myself what I had known was true for a long time. I needed help. And I was afraid to ask for it.

I thought that Karen had betrayed our friendship by causing me so much pain, but in reality she did more for me than any friend I've ever had. It sounds cliché, but she saved me from myself, and for that, I'm thankful. And in the end, I did the feminist thing. I helped *myself*.

Rebecca wrote the following poem as a reflection after a visit to see her father in Hawaii. As her work shows, Rebecca's expectations of Hawaii and of the visit, were quite different from what she found. I especially like this poem because I can see Rebecca's sense of self developing in relation to her surroundings and her family.

MAUI YEAR 2001

Rebecca Guest, 15

BIRACIAL

Where I am doesn't seem real
Surrounded by cardboard boxes
Resembling the homes of a suburban villa
Standing straight, tall and identical like soldiers
Each his own freshly watered lawn
And black tin mailbox

My eyes dart to a lone plant
A tree marked with a rouge "X"
Something real
This tree is so different from any on the mainland
Its leaves long and narrow, formed a shelter for children
That once frolicked around its jagged trunk
The only thing in eyeshot that resembles a postcard sent out from
    this modern-day paradise

And yet on that postcard there was no "X" on the tree

And no greasy fast-food smell or seven-story "skyscrapers" which
    protrude a thick smoke

That made the sky a glossy pink
No, THAT postcard talked about blue skies, sea salt air,
And wishing *you* were here
Also mystical towns with names that roll around in your mouth:
Lahaina, Kihei, Paia
But when I visit these mystic ports all I see are
Dayton, Springfield, and Fairborn.

Even Yellow Springs was found lurking in upcountry,
Along the base of the giant lava chamber, leaking from
    somewhere near the mountain's pinnacle,
Lies a little town where on vacation known faces from all over
    the world compete or relax
Depending on the person
I check in to the shops
Looking for "authentic" Hawaiian garb:
A coconut bra
Unfortunately the universe is not with me
For as I try shop after shop
With no success whatsoever
I frequently hear similar phrases
About growing up in a town identical to this

Can you believe it?
Halfway across the Pacific Ocean
There is a town that actually says it's lost in the '60s
I gotta get out of here

There is hope
Aboard a bouncing catamaran
I feel joy known to no others
I am chasing dolphins
With my hands in the water
I can almost feel their slick, shiny skin

One releases wastes
I quickly pull my hand back out of the water
But put it back in
Remembering this is a once-in-a-lifetime chance
I can also wash it later

This is just like a dream
Hazy, like heaven
With its cardboard houses
Lined up like soldiers
Each his own freshly watered lawn
And black tin mailbox
Also a tree planted in every garden
This time without an "X"
Reminding us of what happened long ago
And what is still here today
aloha

One of the challenges I face is figuring out how best to carry on the memory of my ancestors. I don't want to forget their struggles, but I also don't want to live in their shadows. I am afraid I am never giving their memory enough justice or that I am not fighting enough to finally fulfill their dreams. I am continually working on being proud of what I accomplish yet also realizing I have much more to do. I am thrilled that my ancestors have helped me so much, but I also know that now is my time, our time, to make a change.

In "I am cara," Cara speaks of how she feels as a child of people who have struggled to survive. She shares how she feels about her role in her family and among her friends. On Cara's shoulders rest the past and the future; she is expected to succeed for the sake of all her family members who suffered.

I admire Cara's acceptance of herself and her sense of connection with those who came before her.

I AM CARA

Cara H. Sandberg, 18

BLACK / JAPANESE / WHITE

I am the child that was given sweet life from the desperation of
    the past of too many lost lives
given to me
I have the expectations of the family of my past
and their lives have been lived
solely for my success
pressure
to see him smile
makes me feel worthy
of the blood
he left on the thick
stiff cotton
which paved his education
and the hardship of his daughter
who was too dark
for the rights she deserved
darker than the paper bag
which is too dark
to be loved to be desired
I am the child and I match the bag
and my friends don't know why I don't tan

and I wonder why they like the cancer
that makes
them the color
of baked leather
the shade that left us oppressed
and they wonder why I snarl
at their ignorance
but that's my history
and the frustration of memory
because remembering is not forgetting

I received many pieces about sex. Some girls spoke out against sex; some girls wrote about their sexual activity. Some said they'd had sex and now have decided not to. Still others wrote that they were not going to until either the time was right or they were married. I respect all of these opinions. I have not yet had sex and I intend to wait until I am ready. I want to make sure that I am able to deal with the responsibilities of having sex. We are growing up in a society in which STDs, AIDS, and teenage pregnancy are common occurrences. Until I am ready to handle the consequences, I am not ready to take the risk.

In the next piece, Monica Sanchez does a wonderful job of describing the emotional side of sex. By explaining her feelings, she shows us that sex can create negative consequences resulting not only in diseases but also in heartache. Similarly, Samantha's piece expresses her own choices and opinions about sex. She shares with us some woman-to-woman advice and hopes that we don't mistake sex for love.

UNTITLED

Monica Sanchez, 17

MEXICAN

I guess I've always known I wasn't the average American kid, girl, teenager, etc. Every time I looked in the mirror I saw that it's impossible for anyone to look at me without noticing my black hair and dark skin. So when I began to get confused about everything, I wondered if this was just "typical" teenage behavior. I figure I'm human before anything else. I'm female, young, and, well, I thought I was in love.

While I'd like to consider myself strong and proud to be a Chicana, sometimes that pride can't help me in certain situations. I hope that sharing my experiences and thoughts about something very personal will help someone or at least me to really dig deep and become a better person.

Ever since I was a little girl I always knew that I was going to save myself until I was married. I hardly knew the concept of what that meant, but I just thought that's what I was supposed to do. Like a lot of young people I grew up pretty naive about sex. All I knew was premarital sex was not allowed in my strict Catholic home, and the consequences were either a baby or STDs. It wasn't until recently when I found out about those other consequences you don't hear about quite as much—the heartache, the stress, the bad reputation, the loss of self-respect, and the loss of trust.

The topic of sex seemed suddenly to just come out of nowhere right around the age of fifteen and never seemed to go away. But I was okay, I mean I was still going to abstain until I got married. After my best friend slept with her boyfriend for the first time, it just made my feelings stronger.

It's not like I wanted to be a nun or anything. I always had boyfriends and liked talking to guys. I started seeing Mike the summer before my sophomore year of high school. It was fun being around him. He made me feel so special. Mike wasn't like the other guys; he wasn't afraid to let me know he loved me and didn't care who knew it.

While I was beginning to fall in love I tried to keep things loose between us. We were such good friends and I didn't want that to end. We became inseparable. I was sixteen, but boy, was I in love. I felt lucky to be with such an amazing person.

Honestly, I can't remember it. It was awkward and we were both scared and I know it was August 11. Besides him saying "this is beautiful" I can't really remember anything else about that moment. What came after is what has made a deep wound in my heart and soul.

I knew a lot of girls who slept around with guys they couldn't remember. I had a friend lose her virginity just for curiosity and afterward became the "easy" target on the guys' list. I knew girls who had slept with their friends' boyfriends, and I knew girls who hadn't slept with anyone but had some of the biggest reputations because they had gone far with guys or were flirts.

But I was different. I had done it out of love, and Mike and I were going to be together forever. Our relationship was going to be sacred. I was still happy. I was definitely disappointed in myself for betraying my beliefs and my family, but it was worth it, I thought. Mike and I shared our love in the most intimate way, and no matter what I did I could never take back that moment.

It wasn't until a month later, when the relationship ended, that the emotional effects of sleeping with the person I loved really hit me. In the first week of October, Mike cheated on me. Although I was only seventeen it was one of the hardest times in my life. I wasn't only recovering from a broken heart, it was more than that. The worst part was I couldn't talk to anyone about it. I hadn't told anyone, not even my closest friend, about losing my virginity. I realize now it was out of shame, but at the time I thought it was out of respect for my relationship with Mike.

I was devastated. I didn't know how to deal with the present—or the future. The thought of sleeping with another guy scared me, and the thought of Mike with another girl killed me. I told him I forgave him and I'd give him another chance. He didn't want me, though. For the next three months he made it clear to me that he wanted nothing to do with me.

There were times when I begged him to give our relationship a chance. He would tell me to shut up. I tried to tell him that in giving myself, I lost everything. He said he never loved me. I felt worthless, betrayed, humiliated, alone, belittled, ugly, depressed. It was so hard realizing that something so special to me didn't mean very much at all.

I've let Mike continue to manipulate me and take advantage of me, but it's getting better. We're still friends (most of the time), and we talk about getting back together, knowing deep down inside that it will never happen. Now I realize that losing your virginity doesn't mean you have to lose your self-respect. For a long time I continued to sleep with him out of lack of self-control and loneliness. I never planned it to end this way.

I'd like anyone out there going through this to know you are not alone. I want a girl out there debating about committing herself to her loving boyfriend to maybe think twice about actually doing it. If you have sex at a young age, it doesn't matter what you look like—if you have a heart, the impact and consequences will have a lasting effect. I know firsthand all about it.

SEX

Samantha McKinney, 17

BLACK

 In life people have to make choices. Sometimes one of those choices could be to have sex or not.

Ladies, I know what it feels like because the first time I had sex I got pregnant at the age of twelve, and the guy that I had sex with didn't even want to be with me. I thought that by having that experience once I would never face something like that again, but I broke my promise and got pregnant again at the age of sixteen. That was a very painful moment in my life, and I had to go through it alone once again.

To me having sex felt like a game. I felt that if I didn't have sex with my boyfriend, he was going to leave me. Then I got pregnant and I learned that was the end of me having fun and all the things that I had planned for my future.

To all you young ladies out there having sex, if your man ever tells you that if you don't have sex with him he'll leave you, you turn to him and say, "If you love me, then you'll wait." Or, you leave and tell him you can do better. Don't lose your virginity over a guy when all he wants is sex, because sex doesn't make you happy.

All those single teenage moms out there, don't think you're fighting this long battle alone. Whatever you do, remember that your life is not based upon what a man wants you to do. Just stay focused on yourself and your child. All those guys out there who call themselves men and think it's all about sex, I just want you to know that it takes a man to be a father. My message to you ladies is that I've been through what you might be facing now, so I want you to know that love, happiness, and relationships are not based upon sex. If you can wait, then maybe it's for the best.

I used to try as hard as I could not to cry. I never wanted to let anyone see me weak or unable to handle things. As I've grown older I seem to have learned that crying is okay. To me it is a natural occurrence that allows us to feel better and more emotionally healthy. I cry with my friends, with my family, and sometimes with complete strangers. I have learned that for me to be a healthy

human who is able to support others, I need to take care of myself and express my emotions. I'm glad that Ka'imi has also realized this, and I hope that others will also realize that it is okay to cry.

MORTALITY

Ka'imi Crowell, 16

HAWAIIAN

It was a beautiful day. Bright blue skies with clean white clouds swirled around like cotton balls, the sun like an overcharged lightbulb. It was a beach day. So some of my friends and I did just that: hit the beach. The ocean was the color of a cerulean Crayola crayon, mixed in with a scribble of teal blue; the fine sand was soft between our toes. It seemed like a perfect day at first.

My friends and I go to a boarding school and live on a campus with stretches of paved roads and many turns. One of my friends decided that, despite the fact that she wasn't old enough, she was going to drive us back. With Blink 182 blasting out of the windows of the light blue minivan and heads sticking out of the sunroof, we sped down the hill. She took the turn too sharply and screeched into a waist-high rock wall.

Needless to say, we all started freaking out a little—okay, a lot. The four other friends who were with us ditched the driver and me, hoping to save themselves from official consequences, as well as the social punishment from being seen in an accident.

When things were finally cleared up, the driver and I sought refuge at this place on campus. We just sat, thinking of what had happened. I was really shaken up. I'd been sitting in the passenger seat, my hand out the window. Had it been hanging inches lower . . . well, we all know how fragile flesh is compared to metal siding, and that van took a beating.

My friend wanted some time alone to think and went to the rec room. I happened upon some guys racing Nintendo Super Mario Karts. One of the guys, a friend of mine, asked what had happened. He and another boy had witnessed the entire incident. I started explaining the story; before I knew it, my eyes began to water. It took a number of pauses to try to collect myself and to prevent the tears from falling. I thought I had to put on a composed mask and look strong, even if I was scared out of my mind inside; that's just the way I am. And just then, the other witness walked over and asked if I was okay.

Those guys don't seem like the type who would care. They were the kind who had to keep that certain detached air about them to save their reputations. But at that moment I looked into their eyes and I knew there was something behind the unconcerned facade.

I've been taught my entire life that tears are a sign of feeling sorry for yourself, that crying means weakness. And I didn't want to come off as self-deprecating or vulnerable. But they taught me something different—that tears only mean that I'm human. They said one thing that night that changed my perspective on everything: "It's okay to cry." And I did.

Jacqueling's piece is one that I struggled with. I love her voice and her writing, but I had problems with the message surrounding black females. It seemed to me that the piece was labeling "ghetto" as a place of ignorance, non-intelligence, and blackness. I didn't know if I should use this piece because to me the book is supposed to uplift and unify girls of color, not persecute them.

However, I later realized that a story like this is not only true but also common. So often I think that girls of color heap blame on one another, instead of praise, when one of us succeeds. We make those who have accomplished wonderful things feel guilty and ostracized. I realized that when Jacqueling says she chose schooling, she does not mean that she is better than others but instead that schooling is the path she has chosen for herself. Jacqueling's piece teaches us that as we see our people succeed we must honor them, and that it is okay to be proud of ourselves. We deserve it.

I Chose Schooling

Jacqueling Nwaiwu, 18
NIGERIAN AMERICAN

As I walked down the crowded halls of Central High on the first day of school, I was overcome with many emotions. I was physically tired because I was not accustomed to waking up so early, and I was also scared and nervous. It was my freshman year, and above all other emotions, nervousness prevailed. I was trembling; my hands were clammy and sweaty. Students were greeting each other. There were clusters of students by lockers chatting away, catching up on all the summer gossip. I continued to walk through the halls observing the madness. Kids were running through the halls playing tag and ramming into each other. Bewildered, I muttered, "So this is high school. It looks more like the circus. So much for thinking that high school is exactly like the preppy, well-mannered students in the weekly TV show *Saved by the Bell*."

I managed to find my homeroom after walking around for fifteen minutes. When I went in, I noticed that over half of the students in my homeroom were students who attended the same junior high as me. I was annoyed with that fact because I wanted to meet new people and make new friends instead of interacting with the same old students from junior high. And with that, I quickly sat down next to a girl with spiky, blue hair, whom I did not know.

Right at that moment, my blond, skinny homeroom teacher, Ms. Larsen, shouted, "Welcome to high school!" She went on, saying, "These next four years will be monumental. These four years will define your character; you will either choose that path of excelling in school or you will decide that socializing with friends is more important. You have two paths to choose from. Today is the first day of school, choose your path wisely."

That statement remained with me for the whole day. I kept thinking to myself, This is the beginning of my high school career, I must do well in school. I must pick the right path.

Attaining a sound education has been my goal since before I could remember. Every day from the time I was in kindergarten to the present, my parents have always said, in their thick Nigerian accents, "Read hard so that you may be successful." (To my parents, "reading hard" is synonymous with studying rigorously.) I have always endeavored to excel in school and a large portion of my motivation is because of that overused quote. Whenever stress mounts, and I feel that I never want to do another paper or another homework assignment, I always remember what my parents would tell me, "Read hard so that you may be successful."

Schooling is crucial to me. I believe that the better one does in school, the more successful he or she becomes in the real world. I define a successful person as one who is happy, has a great family, and has a great-paying job.

Over the course of the year, every student in my homeroom chose either to take school seriously or to slack off. In homeroom, cliques started to form. The slackers sat on one side of the room, while the studious, grade-conscious students sat on the other side. Students on the slacker side of the room constantly yelled and were rowdy, while the students on the grade-conscious side of the room were busy trying to study or complete homework.

One day, I came into homeroom and sat in my designated spot: the studious, grade-conscious side of the room. The morning announcements were blaring while I frantically tried to complete my homework.

I was completing my math problems when suddenly the bell rang, indicating that it was time for first hour. I ignored it and continued to finish the problems due that hour. Before I knew it, the second bell rang and I was late for math class.

I quickly jammed my books in my bag and ran out of my fourth-floor homeroom. I ran down the hall and up the stairs to the fifth floor. When I got to the fifth floor, I was blocked by a group of African American girls. The five rowdy girls stood in the entrance of the stairwell. I was so agitated. I wanted to push the girls out of my way so I could get to class. But instead, I maneuvered through the crowd. As I was doing that, one of the girls loudly said, "Who do she think she is anyway, huh?" The group of girls roared with laughter. Another girl said, "Ya'll leave her alone. She trying to get her an edga-macation." And with that, everyone laughed even more. I turned around and looked at them, but said nothing. I simply walked to my math class humiliated.

At that moment, I strongly regretted running down the halls like some geek. I strongly regretted not saying something to them. I strongly regretted having the intense desire to go to my math class and do well in school. It was as if the girls were saying, "Who do she think she is, huh? A black girl trying to be white. An oreo, black on the outside, but white on the inside. Do she think she betta than us? She betta not, 'cause she ain't. School ain't that important for her to be running like that to some class. Some black girls don't know their race. Education ain't all that important. I'd rather clown wit my homies than run to class actin' like I'm white tryin' ta git an education."

"Who she think she is anyway, huh?" I was furious. What exactly did she mean by that! I was only trying to get to class. Excuse me if school means a little more to me than "hangin' out wit da homies." I couldn't believe I gave those girls so much power that they were able to ruin my day.

The next day, I went to homeroom. I mentioned the story to Meg, the girl with the spiky, blue hair. Meg said, "Forget them.

School is more important than trying to fit into some popular clique. Look at me. I have blue hair. I try not to fit into groups who don't accept me for me. School is much more important. Don't waste your energy on ignorant people."

Right as she said that, everything was clear. I didn't have to waste my energy on them. I chose schooling over socializing. I chose to study for tests instead of "gossiping over someone's baby's mamma." I selected education over ignorance. I thought to myself, Maybe I am not "ghetto" and maybe I do choose to speak properly. I am not any less black; I am just being me. I preferred work over play, homework instead of fitting into a crowd where I don't belong. I chose schooling.

When looking back at the experience I had with those girls, I thank God every day. That particular experience reaffirmed my goal, which was to attain a sound education. I thank God for giving me the initiative to select the right path, despite all odds.

As far as religion goes, I have never really known what to believe in. I was raised Unitarian Universalist, but I never felt that it taught me much about spirituality. When my mother married my stepfather, he introduced us to his way, traditional Lakota spirituality, which differs immensely from Christianity. I feel fortunate to have had the chance to be exposed to more than one belief system.

Still, I have many questions. I wonder whether we are actually creatures of a higher being, or if we are just alone? Are our actions really watched, or do we affect only ourselves? And most of all, are we judged; if so, by whom, and how do we know what the outcome is? I don't know if my questions will ever be answered. But I am amazed by—and slightly envious of—people of very strong faith.

In the next piece, Leah speaks of how she came to believe in a traditional Indigenous Creator instead of the Christian God; I can relate to her writing because I have learned a little about both of the paths she describes. While many people of color choose Christianity, I believe it is empowering for us to embrace our own spiritual traditions.

GOD VS. CREATOR

Leah Skjefte, 15
OJIBWE

For years I was told to believe in the Christian God for one reason: If I didn't, I would go to hell. While teachers at my religious school were busy making me completely afraid of this "superior being," family members were introducing me to the Ojibwe culture's traditional Creator. It was very confusing for me to try to understand both higher powers at the same time. After a few years of deep thought and confusion, I stopped believing in God and made a personal choice to believe in the Creator.

By the age of ten, fear of going to hell wasn't enough of a reason to believe in God. How did I come to this conclusion? My sister started joking around, teasing me that God didn't really exist. That's when I started to ask questions.

I spent the next few years asking questions like: If God is so powerful, why did He have to take a nap on the seventh day before He got around to making rules for us? Why did He need all these rules if He made us in his image in the first place? Why does He want to send us to hell for stealing something as little as a Popsicle? Why is it that all these people are telling me to have faith in God not because of the good and joy He could bring us, but because of what terror will come if we don't?

In Sunday school, I kept asking, "Why?" We were told, "Slide over in your chairs and make room for Jesus!" So I asked the teacher, "If Jesus was one person when he was alive, how can he be with everyone at the same time now?" "Because he can," the teacher said. "He's Jesus."

I went to a Lutheran school when I was young, and whenever we did something the teacher didn't approve of, like not paying attention in class, we would have to wear a wooden cross on a really itchy string around our necks. I doubt Jesus really cared if I was paying attention in class or not; the teacher was just using God to punish us for what she thought was wrong.

Meanwhile, my parents brought my sister and me to powwows. My mom made jingle dresses for us, and we danced together. I had the best time. I could see how much fun it was for everyone. My parents even had a hard time getting me to leave . . . unlike Sunday school.

My parents were introducing me to a new religion, if you will, by taking us to powwows. I didn't know much about the spiritual importance of powwows, but, somehow, I could understand it. I felt whole when I was there or when I listened to powwow music at home. This was a feeling I never got from the "God" part of me. So at the same time I was asking questions like, "Why did God give us hate if he wants us to love our fellow human beings?" I was reading books, thinking about and being told stories of the Creator. It was all coming together. Even though I was afraid to not believe in God, I was believing more in the Creator.

Oddly enough, when I made my choice to believe in the Creator and leave God behind, I realized I had already made that choice a long time ago. It was just that the fear of what would happen to me if I did not believe in God made it difficult for me to say, even to myself, that the Creator was it for me.

I chose to believe in the Creator because it makes more sense. I don't need to ask questions like, "Why does the Creator do that?" The Creator just feels right. Perhaps this is because I don't feel as if I am being forced to believe in this higher power, or as if I am being lied to.

At a young age I was forced to believe in a religion that I didn't understand. At the same time, I participated in another that I had never really known about. Throw in years filled with confusion and some patches of fear, along with unanswered questions, and all this adds up to who I am today.

Am I sorry that this is how it all happened—how I came to believe in the Creator? No. Do I hope other teens reading this feel better about their own religious confusion or decisions? Yes. Do I hope parents stop sending their kids conflicting messages on spirituality? Yes.

"*Entry to Church*" *by Jolynne speaks of a faith so strong that it provides a shield from pain encountered in a spiritual environment. Her piece brings up issues of race—and issues of anger and forgiveness. What I found most inspiring is the strength Jolynne receives from her faith.*

ENTRY TO CHURCH

Jolynne Gonzalez, 16

HISPANIC

I enter through the long tunnel . . . so so dark.
The light is coming; it's not that far.
Ouch! That seriously hurt me—a pain in my side.
How convenient is that in this spirituality?
He is not the white man I had in mind to see,
nor did I ever imagine that he would seek to harm me.
Excuse yourself, girl!

Those words echo in my ears.

They make me want to crumble and break out in tears.

He thinks he is better than me.

So what?

I don't care . . .

I know he is wrong and I wonder,

what religion do we share?

As the light reaches my face, the altar becomes clear.

My fear, once great, has now completely disappeared.

I see my savior hanging, a symbol for all to see

and I accept this fate of mine,

as colored as I may be.

My life will have strong meaning.

My faith will long endure.

No matter how many rude men I meet.

No matter how naive they can be.

No matter how long the dark tunnel is.

No matter anymore.

My skin may be my burden.

This is something that will always show.

Just like the blood pouring out from his wounds.

I look to him for strength and his angels will provide,

even through my suffering, when I mourn.

This is my mantra and that man . . . will hurt me no more.

For as long as there is God in my life, He will be my

eternal and spiritual sword.

With my love I will bring peace.

With my happiness I will spread the joy.

With my soul I will connect to all.

With my kindness I will kill.

The light will be my guide and I hope I am never led astray.

My life will have strong meaning.
My faith will long endure.
No matter how many rude men I meet.
No matter how naive they can be.
No matter how long the dark tunnel is.
No matter anymore.
With my love I will bring peace.
With my happiness I will spread the joy.
With my soul I will connect to all.
With my kindness I will kill.

I am a feminist because of my mother. As far back as I can recall my mother has fought for women's rights and instilled in me independence and a strong sense of self. I remember when I was five years old, reading children's stories with my mom as she became furious because once again the bad person in the story was a female. I remember her lectures on how I should never allow a man to rule my life and her insistence that I have a good career and make myself happy. I remember attending feminist marches with her and together chanting for women's rights.

Her influence has been lasting. I've taken to heart the struggle for women's rights and rights for all oppressed groups. My mother's strong feminism created a spark inside of me that has made me now realize what my true passion is. I owe my mother so much and I thank her immensely for instilling in me a fighting nature and a longing for social justice.

Like me, Cecilia was also strongly influenced by her mother, although in a different way. Her own independence and feminism were a result of her mother and her mother has helped her more clearly define her own path in life. Both Cecilia and I owe a lot to our mothers.

BEHIND THE WHEEL

Cecilia Nguyen, 15
VIETNAMESE

Since the fifth grade, teachers have slapped questionnaires on my desk to fill out. "What do you want to do when you grow up?" popped up on every one, and I've always answered "pediatrician." I had envisioned myself sipping an espresso at a café across the street from Central Park while looking over one of my patient's records. Doctorate degrees would line my sparkling Manhattan apartment walls. Years of television created dreams like that. Naive little girl from ol' Oklahoma attempting to make it in the Big Apple. It was wishful thinking, trying to model my life after *ER*.

Truthfully though, it was much more than that. The honor that went with an M.D. attracted me. Most importantly, it provided a chance to break the stereotype that surrounds me as a first-generation Asian American girl in my family. I have noticed a scarce supply of Asian doctors in Oklahoma. Pharmacy is a popular major for Asians. Orientals have taken over Wal-Mart pharmacies across this state. Counting millions of pills does not appeal to me, no matter how high the salary is. I need adventure with some variety. Emergency medicine as portrayed on *ER* seems to fulfill that craving. Split-second decisions, high tension suffocating everyone, and the stench of body fluids attracts me.

Every time I scrub my bathroom toilet while my little brother plays a video game, I seethe about the way society views the position of girls. Why do parents teach their daughters to cook, clean, and sew instead of their sons? If my parents taught me plumbing and auto mechanics with the traditional skills expected of females, I would accept them because I know that they are preparing me for a life on my own. No parents do that, though. It is as if they were training girls to be housewives who depend on their husbands to do the dirty work. If I am already cleaning the toilet, why not let me plunge my hand into it?

I have not always been this bitter about the way the world works. Blame my feminism on my mother. She lived the model life of a homemaker straight out of a '50s sitcom. While she earned a degree in computer science, my mother devoted herself to staying home with her children. Mom dedicated so much of her life to my little brother and me that she changed my view of the society with one little phrase. It came about when my mom was driving me to the mall to do some mother-daughter bonding.

Clicking her right turn signal, she blurted out, "You and Jacob are all I live for."

Instinctively, I squeaked out a "thanks" with the words still echoing in my mind. When it settled in, I asked, "Why, Mom? That is just wrong."

I sensed that bewildered eyes were behind her sunglasses. She shrugged and moved the subject of conversation to the latest sale at Dillard's.

Of course I was touched by her words, but they created a paradox for me. I thought that my mother deserved more than having only two kids to live for. What will happen to her when we leave for college? Will she sit at home alone or perhaps buy cats to keep? I'm hoping that she will join the work force.

Watching my mother for fifteen years molded me into who I am. But I don't want to turn out like her. She breezed through high school; I am going to graduate numero uno in my class. While she went to Central State University, Harvard, here I come. Mom lived in small-town Oklahoma; New York will overwhelm me. She married young while I will never marry. She became a homemaker; I will become a doctor.

Taking my first spin around the block, my mother and I had our usual "talk."

"Oh my God!" my mother squirmed as I backed out of the driveway. "Did you not see that car behind you?"

"I saw it! It was far away!"

"You have to remember that objects in the mirror are closer than they appear."

I smiled sheepishly, "Oh yeah. Okay."

"God, you're a stupid driver. You will never drive like me."

I snorted, "Mom, I will never do anything like you. Now let me do it my own way."

In tenth grade I had two friends who were pregnant. One decided to keep the child and one was going to have an abortion. I tried to be there for both of them, but I found it hard, because I simply could not relate. I had never even thought of having a child and planning on what to do with one seemed even harder.

My friend who decided on abortion went through with it and went on with her life. It was hard because I knew she was suffering, but I felt that there was really nothing I could do. My other friend who wanted to keep her baby ended up having a miscarriage. Both were in pain, not only physically but mentally. Their life plans had been halted and they were forced to deal with a decision that could change the rest of their lives.

As I realized how these girls' plans had changed, I thought about how nothing is really set in stone in our lives. So often I feel that I know what I will do and I know how things will go, but I am also not sure. How do I really know what the future will bring me? I think Camille feels the same way. In her beautiful piece "Plan C," she shows how real life forced her to alter her plans. Another story written by a young woman who wishes to remain anonymous tells what it was like to have an abortion and the feelings she has surrounding her decision. Both stories show the effects of pregnancy and the feelings that go with it.

PLAN C

Camille Hoosman, 17
AFRICAN AMERICAN

I was sitting in Ms. Kahn's second-grade classroom with my best friend, Tsion. She was a very light-skinned girl with long black hair that flowed down past the middle of her back. It was always neatly braided into two ponytails, complemented by beautiful hair accessories. My hair stopped just below my shoulders and was usually pulled back into one ponytail. My skin was the color of chocolate, and I was quite skinny. We proudly paraded around school in our plaid uniforms and were the first to wear white socks with our dresses instead of the navy or maroon socks that we were supposed to wear. We were two of the smartest girls in our class and spent much of our time telling secrets to each other. We decided that we would write a story about the future, the story of our lives.

Tsion and I, only seven years old at the time, had thoroughly planned our futures and were busy writing our story. We had a shiny red spiral notebook, two pencils, and a great deal of imagination. Everything was actually quite well planned. We were going to Paris for college, after which we would get married to gorgeous men and own million-dollar mansions. We wouldn't have maids, but butlers instead, and after working and shopping, any leftover time would be spent vacationing at various locations. All of this would be made possible by the profits turned over by our billion-dollar corporations. I would have two children, while she would have three, and that was exactly how it was going to be. Things would be precisely the way we had planned them. That was simple enough, right?

It's funny how plans change.

After the sixth grade, we attended different schools, and I kept the notebook. It rested on a shelf in my room, and we would read through it from time to time. By then we had realized that our plans were somewhat unrealistic. We probably wouldn't have billion-dollar corporations, and neither one of us could understand one word of French, so we were content to attend college in New York while seeking our fame and fortune. Tsion would attend Julliard because she loved to dance, and I was undecided on which college to attend, but I was certain that I would be in New York when our outstanding talent was finally discovered. That was our new plan, our plan B.

It's funny how plans change.

More time passed, and when I was fifteen I met a guy named Eric. He was eighteen and very persuasive. With a few smooth words and the softest touch, he had successfully stolen my most valuable treasure. And five months later, I could no longer deny what I had been trying to force out of my mind for the previous few months. I couldn't ignore it anymore, because for the first time, I felt it kick. What was I going to do now? How would I tell my parents? What would people think of me? I cried night after night, but only when I was alone. During the day, with the other people around, it was easy to forget about my problems, hide the truth, and wear my mask. But at night when I was all alone, I had to face the truth. I had to think about what I was going to do. All the while, I kept my secret to myself. Not even Tsion knew.

This time it wasn't funny.

My secret finally came out in early January, and on April 27, 1999, my baby girl was born. I named her Ava Renee. I never planned to have a baby as a teenager, and a lot of things were different after April 27. I knew that my life would be much more difficult than it had been before. I knew that it would be a struggle to stay in school and reach my goals. I knew that people would look at me much differently than they had before. I knew that I would be stereotyped as "a girl with a baby." And I knew that many boys wouldn't want to date me because I had a child. I realized that once again my plans would change. But I also knew that I loved her more than anything else in the world, more than myself.

So now, I'm on to my next plan.

I made a new plan for myself. It was not at all like my selfish second-grade story. My revised plan included the both of us, my daughter and me. I decided that I wouldn't let this one setback ruin the rest of my life, or better yet, the rest of our lives. And although I have no idea what will happen, I know that I have to stay strong for the both of us. I plan to finish school. I plan to always be there for my daughter. I plan to be successful in the career of my choice. This new plan of mine is just a basic blueprint with room for additional plans. I'd like to think that this is my final plan, but maybe there's never a final plan. Maybe things never quite work out the way that they're planned. Maybe eventually, I'll learn to stop planning. But for now, I'm on plan C.

UNTITLED

Anonymous, 19

BLACK

I had heard that when a woman gets pregnant she just knows. And I did. I just knew that I was pregnant. For about a week or so I had felt my body changing. My breasts were getting harder and I felt really bloated. But nothing is true until it is confirmed by facts. So I talked myself into going to Walgreen's to buy a home pregnancy test.

Buying the e.p.t. two-pack wasn't as scary as I thought. I was embarrassed though. The cashier didn't know it, but I was totally single. I wasn't in a long-term, loving relationship of any sort. To be perfectly honest, I wasn't sure who the father was. Well, that's not entirely true. My ex-boyfriend had visited me about three weeks prior, and I'd been sleeping with my current interest about a month and a half, so I knew it could only be one of the two. However, at this point my pregnancy was not a fact, it was simply a hypothesis. One that I hoped would be disproved after taking the test.

I remember the words on the back of the e.p.t. box perfectly. Let the test rest for a full minute. If two pink lines appear, you are pregnant. If there is only one, you are not. After that "full minute" I sat on the bathroom floor in shock. Why won't that second line go away? I thought. So the hypothesis had been confirmed: I was pregnant.

It's amazing how fast the human brain works. Seriously, I went from, "Shit, I'm pregnant," to "I'm going to have an abortion," in like three seconds. I never went through that "God is going to hate me. I'm going to hell for killing an unborn child" crap. As far as I was concerned (and I still believe this), I was nineteen years old and barely able to take care of myself. How could I expect to take care of someone else? Call me selfish, but having a child would not be fair to me. I wasn't ready to leave school, move back home, and live with my parents. I wanted to party, have a good time, and meet new people—not change diapers and cajole a child.

So the next day I did something that I should've done when I first started having sex. I called Planned Parenthood. It's sad but remarkably convenient how they handle calls like mine. There's an automated system that says, "Press one for abortion services," and an attendant tells you what you need to bring, when to be at the clinic, and on what day. There were no hassles or questions about anything. Hell, they were quicker than a fast-food service. I was off the phone in ten minutes.

A week later I was in the Planned Parenthood office with my best friend and four hundred and five dollars. This process wasn't quite as fast as I would've liked, but considering the nine-month alternative, the time flew by.

I talked to a counselor and we discussed birth control and how I could prevent this from happening again. She told me stuff that I really already knew but for some reason hadn't put into practice. By this time I had narrowed down the root of the problem to having unprotected sex with my ex. She asked, "Does the father know?" I told her not yet. At that point I wasn't really sure I wanted to tell him. I knew he had the right to know, but still I felt uncomfortable disclosing the whole story to him. It's strange, really. I felt that since he and I were no longer together as a couple, he didn't need to know what was going on in my life. And what if he got mad that I didn't tell him before I decided to abort? At that point I didn't care. I just wanted it to be over. But in the next few days I thought about it and came to the conclusion that he needed to know.

The actual abortion didn't hurt. This was partly because I chose to be sedated but also because I was only one month along. I spent the next few days in bed and on the couch watching television. I returned to school and my normal life.

I don't feel any post-abortion remorse because I know that I made the right decision for me at this point in my life. Despite not regretting my decision, I do regret putting myself in that position. I had sex education in grade school, high school, and from my parents—there was no reason for me not to use birth control. Not only that, but not using a condom every time was stupid. I'll be honest. I thought, "This one time without it won't hurt anything," but it did. It almost cost me my future and who knows what else.

If I had to give one tip based on my experience, I'd say that if you're afraid to go to Planned Parenthood and take care of your birth control needs, then you shouldn't be having sex. It's that simple. If you can't be responsible for yourself and you're not in an emotionally stable state to raise a child, don't have sex. I don't think I was ready for a sex life when I created one for myself. And my lack of preparation almost manifested another human being.

*R*ubi's piece is enchanting. The way she describes the spirit, herself, and Africa is captivating and surreal. Her poem displays a sense of maturity, understanding, and splendor.

SPIRIT KEEPS HER

Rubi Vaughn, 18
AFRICAN AMERICAN

she went to question the horizon
looking and waiting and trying to

improve herself only to be
misunderstood, underestimated and stifled
by the grim and gray
surroundings

she keeps going
sometimes almost wishing
to stop.
and end.
all things
and sink into her body.
she cannot.
spirit keeps her thinking.
spirit keeps her dreaming.
spirit has no name to her.
she cannot see it or hear it
but she can feel it.
it is older than anything
never touched or seen.
older than time, matter and
space
thank Goodness for Goodness

blue dreams scribbled with
magic colors
me me me me me
wish

my soul is nodding off now
heavy eyed and beginning to
dream of AFRICA.

she's beginning to
black out the light

naked body in
fetal position.

i'm fast asleep now
dreams of AFRICA make my soul
twitch
and squirm
pregnant with the Mother

exodus of the soul.

body blurred
and beginning to burn.

she rises to the wind.

SHARING OUR SORROWS

As I began receiving submissions for this book, I was surprised by the number that addressed pain and loss. Many girls shared stories about parents dying or loved ones being killed. Others told about depression, anger, and abuse.

What amazed me the most was the tremendous amount of pain these girls encountered. Perhaps because we, as girls of color, are oppressed by race and gender, our pain is somehow magnified. When we are depressed, we are still forced to see ourselves on television as sex objects and criminals. When we are mourning a death, we are still hearing racial slurs. When we experience violence in our neighborhoods, we still face discrimination in the workplace.

While our pain cannot and should not be compared to that of others, we should strive to recognize it in ourselves and others, and to support one another. Sharing Our Sorrows is not meant to bring people down, but instead to prompt us all to recognize these stories and the pain that surrounds them. By sharing our sorrows we can support each other and slowly begin to heal.

~

When I was five my great-grandmother died. I went to the funeral with my mother and our other family members. I had never really gotten to know her, so the loss was not as significant to me as it was to the others. However, at the cemetery I began to realize how lucky I really was. I remember looking up at my mother and seeing her crying. I couldn't even begin to imagine how she was feeling. At that age I was unable to fully contemplate the effects death had on people. All I really understood was that death is a powerful experience for all those involved; that may have been the only thing that I needed to know about death.

I received many pieces of writing on the topic of death, a subject that has affected many teenage girls of color. I'm sorry that I was unable to include all the pieces, and I wish to offer my gratitude for all the stories and my sympathies for the experiences. The first piece, by Shatara, describes the death of a grandparent. Many girls experience the natural passing of an elderly relative, and it is often our first brush with death. In this way, perhaps experiencing a loved one's death is one of the inevitable passages we must make on our way to adulthood. Shatara captures the powerful emotions that accompany the death of a family member.

DEATH OF A GRANDMOTHER, LOSS OF A FRIEND

Shatara Miller, 12
AFRICAN AMERICAN

It was between the years of 1999 and 2000 that everything was going perfectly. Or was it? Everyone was so excited about the upcoming holidays. But then my grandmother got sick and no one knew what sort of sickness she had. After a few weeks to a month, we found out that she had some sort of cancer. We visited her every day at the hospital, and the doctors said that she might not make it. Everyone was heartbroken.

One day I went to visit her. We were just talking and all of a sudden she started throwing up. I jumped off the bed and backed up into the curtain that separates the two bedrooms. She said, "What's the matter, punkin, you scared?" She looked so helpless, and I felt bad because there wasn't anything that I could do for her but stand there. She was lying in bed sick, coughing with teary eyes and a handful of tissue. She was pale and her feet were starting to swell. Her eyelids were heavy, and her lips were shiny and pink, and she was always feeling cold. These were the symptoms that she'd had before she was diagnosed, so we knew that she wasn't getting any better.

Just a day before Thanksgiving, going on Christmas, she died. I found out at school the next day, and things were never the same again. Several months later, I graduated from elementary school, and my grandmother couldn't be there to share the joyous moments with me.

There will always be an empty space inside of me because my grandmother is not here, but I will always remember her, especially her voice. It was like a whistle blowing in the morning breeze. So soft and sweet, yet so powerful but calm. Like when I used to go to the store and bring something back. Then I would offer her a piece of what I had, but she'd say, "Nah." Then she would say, "Punkin, let me get a little piece, let me taste that." I'd give her some and then she would want it all, but I didn't mind because I would share with her like she shared her love with me.

The following pieces, by Christina and Michelle, show the strong effects that a violent, untimely death of a family member has on a girl's life. Each girl writes of her pain and how, following the experience, she is ultimately better able to make decisions in her own life.

It's hard for any of us to cope with the reality that young people are killed by gunshots, and I cannot imagine what the pain would be like for someone in their family.

THE DEATH OF A LOVED ONE

Christina Carrillo, 15

HISPANIC

It all started on June 8, 2000. I was sitting down on my cousin's bed waiting for my sister to do my hair. My cousin, Louie, walked into the room and asked who I was waiting for.

A few minutes later my sister showed up and said, "Let's get you ready for that big dance."

My cousin, Louie, was really excited for me. When I was ready, he told me I looked like a queen. My mom took pictures of Louie, my sister, Marcy, and me. When my date picked me up, Louie asked him questions, like, "How old are you? What's your name? What's your phone number?" As I walked out of the house with my date I had a strong feeling in my heart telling me to stay home. As if something was going to happen. But I just ignored it and left.

My date and I arrived at the dance at six o'clock. I was having a great time dancing with different friends and talking to many people. After dancing I took pictures with my date and we drank some beverages. Half an hour later when Louie's favorite song came on, I just had to call him so he could listen to it. We listened together to the song until it finished; then we hung up. Afterward, my friend Randy asked me out to dance. So I went with him. All of a sudden I just stopped dancing and Randy asked me, "What's wrong with you? Are you okay?"

I looked at him and started crying. I told Randy, "Something's wrong. I know something's wrong with Louie. I could feel it in my heart. I don't like this feeling, Randy, I'm so scared."

He looked at me and told me, "Don't worry about him. He must be at home kicking it."

When the dance was over, I went straight to the car and told my mom I just wanted to get home. As I arrived to the house I tried to forget about the feelings inside me. I picked up the phone to call my boyfriend Steven. As I touched it, the phone rang and I answered it. "Hello!"

"Christy, call your mom now." My aunt sounded devastated.

Then I asked her, "What's wrong? Did anything happen to somebody?"

"Just get your mom and hurry up!"

I gave the phone to my mom and told her that it was Oralia, my aunt.

I was scared because of the way my mom looked. When she got off the phone, I asked what was wrong. Then she told me and my sister that Louie had been shot. We couldn't believe it at first. But we started panicking. We all got our stuff and left for the hospital. When we got to the hospital we all ran to the emergency room.

Inside the emergency room the doctor came to us and told us that Louie had died a few minutes before we got there. My aunt told us that his last words were, "Just remember that I'll be watching over all of you and tell Auntie, Marcy, and Christy that I love them all and that I'm going to a better place. I'll never forget none of you."

I couldn't believe it at all. I started crying hysterically. Everyone was crying and the priest was praying. I didn't want to go home. I wanted to stay with my cousin. My mom had to take me with her. When I got home, I couldn't go to sleep. I was just thinking about my cousin's death. I went straight to the little room where we all used to play together, crying my heart out. I still couldn't believe it.

Two weeks later they had the wake for him. I was there with my family, practically dying inside of sadness and anger. There were a lot of people at the wake, especially a lot of his homies. My boyfriend had been one of Louie's closest friends and was right beside me the whole time.

The day of the burial, everyone was there. I couldn't stand looking at my cousin being put underground. I felt like jumping in there to be with him forever. Days later I just couldn't concentrate on my work. I just kept thinking about Louie's death. All I do is think about him, day and night. But I know he wouldn't want me to cry for him. He would want me to get on with my life, and that's what I plan to do. I'm going to reach all of my goals and become someone in the future for him. His death inspired me to go on with my life and make positive changes. I feel as if I'm doing it for him and for myself.

Untitled

Michelle Stevenson, 15
AFRICAN AMERICAN

I was sitting in my house and I noticed a halo over my older brother's head. When he passed me, I could feel this rough and cold wind. I screamed and yelled at my mom, telling her not to let him leave. I grabbed hold of his leg and then this power—I don't know what it was—pushed me off him. He bent down and said, "I love you and I'll be back, Meechie." I told him, "No, you won't, don't leave." About four or five hours passed and a policeman knocked on our door and told my mom that my brother Maurice had been killed.

After that day I had this taste in my mouth that wouldn't go away. It felt like I had bitten into a bone and my teeth had disintegrated in my mouth. I could feel nothing but rough ends as I took each step to my bus stop.

The worst part of the whole thing was my mom. She said she understood, but she didn't. She said I was too young to go to the funeral. I didn't think so. I just wanted to see his face one more time. I cried and cried as my mom and dad slipped on their black funeral wear. I even tried to put on the dress that Maurice had helped me pick out for church. My mom took the dress off me and told me I wasn't going. I screamed at her in my loudest voice, "He wants me there, Mom. He wants me there!" As I broke down in tears, I remembered him, sitting and talking with me about my day at school, and the time that I had chicken pox and he was the only person I would let put calamine lotion on me. My parents left anyway. Soon after I sat in Maurice's room and began to look at pictures. For hours I cried. I'll never forget the first couple of weeks.

A few years passed. I had coped with my pain by fighting, stealing, and basically doing everything wrong. My teachers said my behavior was a big change; I had never acted like that before. I had my first run-in with a county detective for stealing a small amount of money from one of my classmates.

I began to make the wrong decisions when it came to friends. I started smoking weed a little too much. I began to drink until I passed out, and when I was drunk I was emotional and violent. I'd talk about my brother, and even though I'd be far away from the house that we used to live in when he died, I'd picture myself there and then my feelings would get worse. I could see him outside his workplace. I could see that man walk up to him and I could feel those bullets puncture his chest. I could see the blood. I could hear his screams. Then my mind would totally flip and I would begin hitting things and screaming, "It's my fault! I let him go. Take me, not him! His kids are gonna grow up without their daddy." But he was already gone.

So here I am, in ninth grade. The beginning of the year was a little hard, but then it began to get easier. I'm doing pretty well now and I have high expectations for myself. I plan to go to Tennessee State College and play for the Lady Vols like my favorite player, Tamika Catchings.

Sometimes at night I'll see if I can talk to him in my dreams, or I'll sit and cry. Every time his birthday rolls around, I give five minutes of silence, and then I begin to cry. I will always remember that taste in my mouth and that feeling of emptiness. I'll also cherish September 23, because that was the date that a great man was born into this world. Maurice, I love you. As long as you stay smiling, I will, too. I'll see you when I get there.

When I first received Ada's piece I was shocked. I was surprised by the violence and the pain she described as well as by the location. I could tell from the zip code that I used to live in the same neighborhood Ada lives in. I remembered feeling unsafe in the neighborhood. But the longer we lived there the more comfortable I felt, because we began to know our neighbors. The idea that this sort of violence occurred there frightened me.

I admire Ada for her story and her ability to share it with us. Ada, you touched me on a very personal level. Thank you.

THE OTHER DAY

Ada Samuel, 13
AFRICAN AMERICAN

You see, it seems like yesterday that the warm summer sun was setting. My friend and I were chilling on the front porch when these two girls came walking down the street. They couldn't have been much older than eighteen, and they looked like trouble.

The closer they got the faster my heart pumped. Then they approached us and before I had time to ask if they needed something I felt the cold gun to my head. The air got thick and was filled with the close smell of alcohol-tainted breath. Everything around me was silent and evaporated. It was just me and the person with the gun. I closed my eyes as tight as I could, knowing I was going to get shot. Then suddenly I heard a loud BANG.

I thought to myself: Oh, no! Am I dead? I looked beside me and I saw my friend lying there in her red pool of death as the two girls ran off.

I dropped to my knees in a flood of tears. Screaming at the top of my lungs, "Help! Anyone!" while praying at the same time for God to spare her life, because it wasn't her time.

Now, today, I cherish life and live it to the fullest because you never know when it might be your time.

Reading Naeesa's piece was incredibly difficult. The way she described the circumstances, the heartache, and the relationship with her stepfather was beautiful and passionate. As I read I thought of my own stepfather. Despite all the many differences that we have had, I don't know what I would be able to do without him. Naeesa's story is about not only a profound loss but a beautiful relationship.

STEVE SAID . . .

Naeesa Aziz, 15
AFRICAN AMERICAN

My mother married Steve about two years ago. I must admit that as much as I wanted to be the proverbial troublesome teenager without a father, I really liked Steve and didn't view the wedding as some sort of funeral. I had heard too many horror stories from friends and relatives about the horrors of life with a stepparent. Steve was a riot, and everyone loved him and his jokes. I believe that Steve became like such a "real parent" to me because I liked him so much, or maybe I was just taught to have a lot of respect for my elders. Whatever the reason, I respected him and through this mutual respect, he understood that he was not totally in control of my life.

I was quite annoyed that morning when Steve woke me up to die. On Sundays I usually woke up around ten o'clock, sometimes even twelve, but this man knocked on my door at eight o'clock. Although I was almost totally sure he woke me up just to annoy me with some trivial story about the restaurant he ate at last night, I sensed something was wrong when I arose from my sleep without the smell of sausage invading my lungs. Steve was diabetic and he had to eat breakfast every morning, so he could take his insulin. No sausage meant no breakfast, and no breakfast meant Steve didn't take his medicine. With this realization, I hastened my step to find Steve bent over in pain, sitting on the edge of his bed.

"Okay," he paused with pain. "This is what's going on." He could only get out about a sentence before another pain stopped him. I was speechless. Since he had gone to the hospital twice earlier that week, I was both worried and a bit unconcerned.

"Wait," he said as he looked to the ceiling with confusion.

"Wait what?" His expression scared me.

"The pains just stopped." He paused again. "I don't know what the hell is going on. Let me just take my medicine and see what happens." He began to lift himself off the bed, and I dutifully followed him into the kitchen.

The moment he sat down at the kitchen table, he was struck by another wave of pain that resonated up through his chest and down through his arms.

This was it. "Call 911," he managed to choke out.

I ran from the table and reached for the phone. I never dialed 911 before. "911!" The dispatcher answered.

"Hello." I guess I was stunned by the urgency in the dispatcher's voice. "My fath—I mean my stepfather is having really severe chest pains." I never had to refer to Steve as my parent before and I saw a slight change of expression in his pained face as I said the word "stepfather."

When the ambulance arrived, Steve decided he was feeling okay again. The paramedics gave him a tablet to chew and I was relieved when Steve said he didn't feel like he wanted to go to the hospital anymore. Despite my relief, I knew Steve, which meant I also knew he felt he could beat anything.

Steve did, in fact, go to the hospital, but I didn't think he wouldn't come back. No one ever told me he died. The river of tears on my cousin's face told me instead. I never wanted to believe it. I told myself that I wouldn't believe it until I physically saw him lying on the table with his eyes in two big X's. I wish death was that cartoon-like.

I did finally see Steve lifeless, and lying on a table, but there were no cartoons around. And when I was told that while the doctors were trying to save Steve, he called out for his baby, his daughter, me, I realized that my father had just died.

Two of my close friends have mothers who have had breast cancer. Both of their mothers made it through chemo and other treatments and have not had problems since. When their mothers experienced this, I always thought what it would be like if my mother were to suffer from such pain, and I have always thought I would not be able to bear it. I depend on my mother so much that imagining life without her is much too difficult.

Christina had to face the reality of losing a parent. She tells of her father's death with sincerity and grace. Thank you, Christina, for casting light on something that many of us have not experienced, and for connecting with those who have.

UNTITLED

Christina Chon, 18

KOREAN

Walking down the hostile hall of the Los Angeles County Hospital, I am overwhelmed by the strong smell of medicine and cafeteria food. The odor pricks my nose and causes a queasy turbulence in my stomach. Following the color-coded tape, which will eventually lead me to the elevators, I notice all types of people: cancer patients, accident victims, janitors, doctors, worried family members, and flower deliverers. Although I am here today visiting my uncle in a different ward, everything around me forces me to remember the first time I was here.

About three years ago, my dad caught a terrible flu. So like most people, my mom took him to the doctor. Little did we know that this doctor's visit would mark the beginning of an endless battle between my dad and the doctors. A few days later, the doctors diagnosed him with liver cancer. My dad, the person I went to whenever I encountered a problem, whether it be academic, physical, or spiritual; the person I depended on for help; the person I sought guidance from not because he was my dad but because he was my friend; the person who calmly understood me yet never once judged me, was dying of cancer.

Within a matter of weeks, I began to experience the cruel reality of death as my dad's health and physical abilities decreased while his pain and suffering increased. However, what hurt me the most was the fact that the doctors or "modern-day medicine" couldn't do anything for him. We (my mom and I) just had to stand by and watch him suffer. Every day was a battle for our family. For my mom, it was the many responsibilities (my dad, housework, and me) she had to juggle; for my dad, it was the literal "fighting for a single breath" physical battle. For me, at the young age of twelve, it was painful to accept the fact that my dad needed to depend on me for simple tasks such as walking, eating, and bathing. During the last several months, my dad weighed about ninety pounds, was bedridden, and could barely eat. As he suffered more, the only thing we could do was increase his intake of morphine. However, despite all the emotional and physical hardships my dad (and my family) endured, my dad never lost his strong faith in God. I personally think that is why I admire him so much. Unlike a lot of people who are facing death, my dad never blamed anyone nor resented God. Through his actions during his last few months, my dad showed me how he had accepted death and was at peace with himself. Watching him pray every day, not for his life but rather for the safety of his loved ones, I realized the importance of the insignificant things we take for granted. Whether it is a parent, friend, nature, or just the fact that we can wake up each morning and look forward to a new day, the things and the people we cherish should always be cherished deep in our hearts.

The idea of life after death wasn't real to me until my stepfather came into my life. He presented the idea that all people die and then their spirits continue to live and are very powerful. On many occasions my family has experienced the presence or the feeling of a spirit.

As other people may speak to God I speak to my ancestors. I fully believe in this connection and know that it is everlasting. In her poem "Spring Breeze," Lisa speaks of her connection with her grandmother even after she has passed away.

SPRING BREEZE

Lisa Carter, 12

BLACK

As the spring breeze blows in the sky
My heart fills with joy. The spirits within the wind
Are dancing around my soul

As the spring breeze blows in the sky
It embraces my skin and caresses my hair.
The spirits are filled with happiness.

As the spring breeze blows in the sky
I am taken away to be reborn again
And the spirit of Catherine comes out to play.

As the spring breeze blows in the sky
I am reunited with my grandmother's spirit above.

As the wind dies
Catherine's spirit remains
For I have felt her touch of love.

My father used to beat my mother. We left him when I was almost two. My mother has never been dishonest with me about his treatment of her; however, I still have yet to fully grasp what happened. I recognize that he abused her, but I'm still confused by how it has affected us, my mother and me, since we left.

*My mother has always been so strong, yet I see his mistreatment of her follow-
ing us wherever we go, and I see myself slowly inheriting it.*

*In "Love Taps," Carlotta writes of a woman being abused by a man. This
piece brings out the bitter truth of what abuse is about and how it claims one's
life. I have yet to really comprehend abuse, both physical and mental, but Carlotta has helped me understand how horrifying it really is.*

LOVE TAPS

Carlotta Smith, 15
AFRICAN AMERICAN

Provider of life
Beat down to shreds
Because she is
The so-called "weaker sex"
Only to feed your ego
To give you power
Because in reality you are nothing
Like a hyena you prey only on the weak women
The ones who will put up with you
Only to be pounded into a corner
With no way out
You keep your dominion
With heart-wrenching threats
Deepening her fear
She no longer has a voice
Or dignity, or a life
Mistreated and beaten
To fill your satisfaction
Why?

She is a woman
The provider of life
Now you want to take hers away.

Sometimes I contemplate my life, my future, and my happiness. It sounds dorky, but before I'm going to sleep or when I'm in class, I'll try to figure out what I want to do. Throughout all of these dreams I have never once imagined what it would be like to not be able to accomplish one of my goals due to a physical disability.

In her short piece, Tallish shares her experience of being deaf. I wish to offer Tallish my support and maybe someday we can sit together and think about our futures.

BEING DEAF

Tallish Bell, 18
AFRICAN AMERICAN

When I was seven I walked with my mom to my new class K-130 at PS 41. They had a program for deaf and hard-of-hearing students.

The moment I sat down on the golden brown chair and looked around at the joyful class, I felt embarrassed.

I looked at the teacher, in her brightly colored clothing, talking to me with a mean face. I could not respond. She screamed at me and I cried with caramel tears falling from my eyes. I could not hear any sounds except the ocean waves with silent voices talking around my ears. I stood there with my fear running all through my body. All I could think about was my future.

Camiele's poem is about a struggling woman who is a single mother, and who, when asked a simple question, hauls off with annoyance, suffering, and bitter frustration.

LATELY

Camiele D. Land, 17
AFRICAN AMERICAN

"What are you doin'?"
Runnin' from my past,
Why do you ask?
You can't help me, Cuz you don't see, the problems I see, kids
    being killed
Crack houses being built,
When will you join in and say YIELD,
Drugs, hatred, crime,
Has been the only thing on my mind,
LATELY
My feet hurt,
Dirt covers my shirt,
But why do you care?
My home need to be cleaned,
My babies need oil sheen, Babies need clothes

Warm food that soothes the soul,
Cryin' for they momma,
Do you deal with that drama?
LATELY
Got no time for my personal stuff,
Gotta bail my brother outta jail,
Go to the post office to get my junk mail,
I'm in a hurry, can't you tell?
LATELY
I'm lookin' for the easy way out,
Cuz I took the hard way in,
Now you come along and ask me, "What are you doin'?"
Trying to survive,
Keep "my people alive,"
That's the only thing that's been goin' on with me . . .
LATELY

When I was younger I used to think that girls of color never got depressed. I thought that it was a white girl's problem, not one that I would ever have.

However, when I became a little older, my self-esteem dropped. When I experienced this, I secretly thought to myself that I must not really be black. I thought that because I had a white mother and she had raised me that I was automatically just having the experience of a white girl.

Now I realize that I was wrong. Girls of color experience the same amount of abuse from society as white girls do, and in many cases even more. I remember looking at a magazine with my weight-conscious friend; she felt sad that she didn't look like the flat-chested, skinny blond on the page. I thought, if she only knew how I felt as I looked at the photographs in the magazine, and saw not only the impossibly skinny bodies but also the white skin, which was common to almost all the models in those pages. Since that time I have tried to stop looking at those magazines.

Today I see how girls of color are portrayed so often in a negative light in our society—or not portrayed at all. While images in magazines and on TV aren't responsible for depression, they do serve as a reflection of our status. It's no secret that women are oppressed by men, and that people of color are oppressed by the dominant culture. And it only follows that those least valued in our society are young girls of color. As a result, I believe we are extremely vulnerable to depression, and to the kind of abuse and lack of support that can result in depression.

The following piece from Yanica is about depression. To all girls who suffer from depression, hang in there, talk to somebody—talk to one of us. We'll be there for you.

DEPRESSION

Yanica Ricketts, 16

JAMAICAN

All alone, I sit in my room. Sad, sorrowful, and filled with despair. There's not a single being who can comfort or console me in this matter. I take my hands and cling to my knees. A liquid form descends onto my cheeks. A million thoughts glide all over my mind. Does the problem lie within me, or is it everyone else? Has the entire world turned against me? I simply can't understand. Why is it that I cannot find happiness or joy? Why am I not loved or at least feel that way? I feel as though I'm being pulled from every angle. So many decisions and choices to make. I consider my options. Should I leave or shall I stay? I know that I can't run because I'll end up where I started. What about death? Is it the answer? Shall it grow to be my refuge? No one knows what I've been through. They can't feel the pain that I'm going through. I'm alone, solitary, and have no one. Where am I? I'm in my depressive phase.

When I was fourteen I fought with my parents constantly. I disagreed with everything they said, and I seemed to be attacked for anything I said. One day as I sat watching the television with my stepdad I got into one of these arguments. Instead of listening to him or trying to voice my opinion, I got up and headed for the bathroom. I didn't know what I was going to do, and I was crying so hard I could barely see. As I stood staring in the mirror I thought about how I hurt. I thought about how I was sick of getting yelled at, and how I just couldn't handle it anymore. As I looked down I saw a pair of scissors sitting by the sink. I had no intention of cutting myself for my own pleasure but instead to make my parents aware of what was happening. I felt as if they didn't know me, that I was too different and that they really didn't love me. As I drew the end of the scissor across my stomach I cried harder and tried to imagine everyone's faces. I could just see my mother crying and saying, "What have you done?" and my stepdad screaming how sorry he was.

In the end, I couldn't do it. I couldn't injure myself just because of an argument. I put the scissors down. I had a small cut but nothing that wouldn't heal soon. I never tried to cut myself again, and for a while I even stayed out of that bathroom because I was scared of the scissors.

I look back on that time with regret but also with sympathy for others who walk further down that path than I did.

Shimere's poem and Precious's story were hard to read. I hope other girls out there realize that what you may be going through is not unusual and that there are people out there who know how you feel.

THESE SCARS

Shimere Etheridge, 14

AFRICAN AMERICAN

These scars
Tell a story
A story not long forgotten
These scars
Speak of a girl
A scared girl
With too much time to think
About what she wasn't
The way you would've
These scars tell a story
Of a girl who thought she was overweight
Of a girl who wouldn't eat
A girl who threw up
A girl who would go on any diet
And exercised constantly
These scars tell a story
Of a girl who couldn't make the grade
Who tried and tried
And never ever made straight A's
Of a girl who wanted to be something
And was told she could never succeed
These scars tell a story
Of a girl who would've done anything for a boy
A boy who would never love her
The way she loved him
Where is he now
When you're standing with the baby in your arms?
These scars are for a girl

Who thinks she is ugly

Because her hair isn't long

Or blond

Because her eyes aren't blue

And because her skin isn't the color of butter

The girl who confuses dark with ugly

These scars tell a story of a girl who wanted to be loved

A girl who would've done anything

For any boy

To hear the words I love you

Of a girl who was given a bad reputation

In the hopes

Of hearing those three words

These scars tell a story

For me

For you

For everyone with a low self-esteem

For every girl

Who wants to be something

She's not

Who looks in the mirror

Who diets

Who thinks she's stupid

Who's never had a boyfriend

Who confuses dark with ugly

Who has done things that have earned her reputation

These scars tell a story

These scars tell my story . . .

And your story

I dedicate these scars on my wrist for all the girls who ever contemplated cut-
ting, for all the girls who cut . . . and to all the girls who died from it. There is

a better way. It's a long journey trying to find it. God bless you on this journey, and God knows I can relate to what you're going through.

UNWANTED

Precious Angel, 14
SICANGU LAKOTA

When I was thirteen I found out how much the world sucked. I found out the meaning of despair. It was one of the saddest times in my life. I was cutting on my wrists and going deeper into the darkness, away from everyone and everything. This is my story.

It started when I felt unloved by everyone. I lived with my aunt and hated her. I was sick of life. My grades dropped and I was failing school.

I walked through the school hall, thinking of how much life sucked. People passing by stared as if I was a freak in a carnival. I walked down the hall with my head down, not wanting to look at people and their evil stares. I wanted to make it all go away. To escape it all. The only comforting thought in my head was to cut on my arms when I returned home. I reached my locker and stood there wondering if I should just go back home. The thoughts in my head were like books in a library, each with its own twisted story. I opened my locker, got out my books, went to my class. I took a seat in the farthest corner. Away from everyone. The teacher hadn't noticed I was even there. I opened my books and flipped to the page where I'd left off writing and drawing. The drawing was of three crosses: one was for me, and the other two were for lost friends and family members.

After my class I walked to my next class. When I sat down in my usual spot, I noticed my notebook was gone. I looked outside in the hall and it wasn't there. I thought that nobody would notice.

Later, some kids came up to me and told me that a teacher had found my notebook and that she took it to the principal. I didn't know what to do. I was totally lost. I couldn't think, I couldn't speak, I didn't hear what anybody else was saying. I just went to my next class. I couldn't think of anything but what they would say about my drawings and the things I wrote.

The counselor called me to his office. I walked there as slowly as I could. I was so scared I was shaking.

The counselor finally called me in and he looked worried. He asked what all the writings were about and the drawings. He said they were gang-related and that he wouldn't get mad if I told him what they were. He saw the picture I had been drawing, the one with the three crosses. I was so nervous I was looking at my feet and fiddling with my pencil.

He asked what it meant, the three crosses and all. I told him they were for my three friends that died. It was all going fine until he got to a poem I had written called "Suicide." I was in trouble. I didn't know what to say. So I didn't say anything. I just sat there. The counselor told me to lift up my sleeve. I refused. I didn't want to. Finally he had one of the lady counselors pull up my sleeve.

I had deep cuts everywhere. Some had scabbed over and some were still open. It looked really bad. They took me to the nurse and had her wash them and bandage them. She asked me why I had done it. I told her and she started crying. She took me back to the counselor's office and said she was done. I didn't know this, but he had called the cops and they were going to take me to the hospital to see a psychiatrist.

When I got to the hospital, I had to wait for thirty minutes. When she finally did come, I could tell by her tone of voice and the questions she asked that she didn't really care. That made me mad.

Later, the cop told me that I would have to tell my aunt. I didn't want to. All she would do is get mad and yell at me. It was a long drive back to our house. By the time we got to the driveway, tears were streaming down my face. I didn't want to go inside. When we walked in, she was pissed off. She asked the cop if I was like this again, could she throw me into jail until my mom came and got me. I was crying now. I told the cop to take me anywhere but there.

After that it was just counselor after counselor. I'm all right now, but about a year ago I was so depressed that I actually turned to suicide. I know other people have the same problems as me, so I thought I would share my story with other teenagers like me.

When I was younger I used to stare at myself in the mirror and wonder why? I wanted to know why I had been chosen. Like some number being picked out of a hat, I had to be the black one in this white city, school, family. I didn't get it. Was I smarter or stronger because of it, or had I been a mistake?

As I grew older I began to look in the mirror in a different way. This time I saw beauty, not only outwardly but within. I saw my own mesmerizing brown skin. I began to love the shape of my nose, my lips, and my eyes. I was proud of myself, my heritage, and what I had to offer. I started to embrace myself.

I am still working on loving me. It's hard at times, but I know deep inside there is a beautiful, shining human being with a great deal of potential just waiting to be seen and heard. I hope that soon all of us will realize this and together we can know that we are amazing and that we will succeed.

The following two pieces are about mirrors. I loved them because of my own experience with the mirror phenomenon—and because through the reflection of our images, mirrors tell us a lot about ourselves.

UNTITLED

Anonymous, 14

LATINA

 When I go to sleep, I always wonder who I am. I face a lot of problems from friends and family. It's hard being a teenager. I have a friend, her name is Michelle, and she has the most wonderful poem. . . .

MIRROR, MIRROR

Mirror, mirror on the wall, who's the one seen by all?
Mirror, mirror in my heart, who's the one playing the part?
Mirror, mirror in my dreams, who's the one not as she seems?
Mirror, mirror in the lane, who wishes she could start again?
Mirror, mirror who I ask, who wants to drop her mask?
Mirror, mirror, I know the reply
Who is it? It is I.

I'm always concerned about my self-image, always trying to impress, and this poem makes me realize that I have to find out who I am before I pretend. Pretending is not the answer since we as Latinas have many opportunities to succeed. We may be seen as a minority, but one day we will be the voice of this country and we need to know who we are before we think that far.

REFLECTION

Nicole Pickering, 17
HAWAIIAN / CHINESE / CAUCASIAN

She just stands there.
Her somber face pale and blank.
The empty stare that took over her usually warm smile.
Never have I seen such sadness,
Never so many tears.
So much pain in just one soul.
Tears fall like a river never-ending,
Sobs continue like sunrise and sunset.
She listens to the broken heart inside her, a broken record playing
    the same song.
She listens to the voices in her head
Telling her, "it hurts!"
All while I look in the mirror
At her.

After I read Mary's two pieces, "Nonsense" and one that appears later in this section, I called her and asked her to tell me more about them.

    Mary explained that she did not write "Nonsense" from personal experience, but instead as a reaction to the situations of some of her friends. She also said that during the time she wrote it, she was in a bad place, and was deeply feeling her own pain and the pain of those around her.

NONSENSE

Mary Standing Soldier, 16

OGLALA LAKOTA

Come to your senses, father said
that's funny I've always felt
all five of my senses
I feel pain, love
I touch my bruised skin
I can also smell cigarette burns
I can see your anger, but I must be blind
because I can never see your happiness
I can hear words, only when I don't cover my ears

*The shortest poems or stories can be the most powerful. Sarah's poem is a clear
example of that.*

THAT CHILD

Sarah Cook, 15

AFRICAN AMERICAN/CAUCASIAN

I care about that child
Who was picked last and left out
Who's different from everybody else.
The one who is alone

Beaten, molested, abused, raped . . .
Unloved . . .
Lonely and depressed.
I care about that child who wakes up
Screaming in the cold, dark night.
I care about that child more than anything . . .
Because that child is me.

I have often been confused about the roots and causes of violence. I know that the oppression that envelops people of color is a major factor in our anger toward people of our own race. We are treated badly by the dominant culture, so instead of retaliating against them, which can be "unsafe," we direct it against our own people.

However, this is not the only cause of violence. Abuse and mistreatment can make a permanent impression when started in the home. My temper is a result of not only how I feel but also how I see my parents and others in my house act as they are upset. Violence and any type of abuse seem to be taught and learned.

By the same token, oppression is taught and learned. Privileged individuals are taught, either subconsciously or not, to have power and to use it to their advantage. The privileged continue to prosper in a system where oppressed groups stay oppressed, and within those groups they damage each other enough that they no longer will need to be lynched, beaten, or overpowered by the privileged. This cycle will continue to repeat itself until one or both groups step out and become aware of the problem.

In "Violence and Abuse," V.M. speaks of how violence and abuse affect her and shows the cycle of abuse at work. Her only expression of how she feels is the anger she takes out on others. I strongly believe that admitting to one's own

anger is the first step in becoming a stronger and better person. V.M. has shown
this, and by sharing her story, I hope she can begin to heal.

VIOLENCE AND ABUSE

V. M., 14

HISPANIC

Violence is around us constantly. You see it on the TV and hear it in the news and radio. I never really want to be violent, but my anger can take hold of me and no one is safe. It is the cause of many tears in my life.

Abuse has become such a part of me that it does not worry me anymore, it does not cause tears. I've seen spousal abuse but I wasn't scared. When my mother was sitting there crying, I tried to show feelings of sadness but felt nothing. My first father was into drugs, and I guess that's what his anger fed on. He and my mom got divorced. I think abuse had a big influence on that decision. My second father, driven by alcohol, also caused emotional scars. Now he is taking care of his problem and he does love us; it is just hard when someone drinks. I see my little brothers crying and scared 'cause of what happens, but for me it has become another part of life, like brushing your teeth. I feel bad about the fact that I will cry if I lose my basketball but do not shed a tear for the pain my mom deals with. I try, but in my heart I know it is artificial. I think I was scared in the beginning and maybe I just grew so strong that it didn't matter anymore.

My anger has been a major problem for me. I take it out on people who do not deserve it, and it makes me feel miserable. I hit people just because I feel like it with no real reason. With brothers, though, one little tug on my hair or one object aimed and thrown at me can cause a storm. I heard on TV that one should count to ten or talk it out, but when I am angry, I just want to hurt the other person so badly. If I do not throw a punch I feel like they have won. They did something bad and got no punishment. It is rage with no thought on how hard I might hit or what it might cause. It hurts terribly afterward. I do not want to harm people, I have shed many tears just by thinking about what I have done.

I have to learn to control myself and set an example. I wouldn't want my children to suffer similar feelings.

"And We Were Gone" is an incredibly powerful piece. Mary told me that she wrote it as a reflection on how she frequently sees Native American grandparents raising their grandchildren because the children's parents are unwilling or unable to care for them. She said she has seen this very often on the reservation, and also within her own family. In Mary's poem she tries to imagine, from the child's point of view, events leading up to a child living with a grandparent.

Mary's poem not only shares an important struggle with us but also reveals some of her own culture.

AND WE WERE GONE

Mary Standing Soldier, 16
OGLALA LAKOTA

Her head sat sideways when she looked at something she could
    not understand
like when dad told mom she could not do anything right

mom would then look at me and shake her head then dad would
    raise and strike
he'd leave all would be silent until he'd come back drunk and
    shatter it
mom would tell grandma to take me for a walk her head would nod
and we'd be gone
before bedtime grandma would sing me a lullaby her voice
    wasn't too good
but it helped drown out the drunken brawls
and the scared weeps
after three years of the abuse
mom got sick not from any flu
but from all the pain
dad no longer would wait
to raise and strike 'til she got him mad
he just would I gave gratitude to solitude
grandma went away a year later
I don't like to say she died because
it sounds like forever, but this way
I know she'll be back to take me
for a walk or sing me a lullaby
she'd take me away from it
all
she took mom away a few months
later but I couldn't leave the law
would not allow it dad was still
alive and they said he could take
care of me
I took mom's place he would
raise and strike me
running away would solve it for only
a little while because I was young
I could not work or be believed
after two years of abuse

I could not get used to the pain
after one night of hurt which
included a bruised face
I gave up life I wanted to leave
forever and never come back
I fell asleep with blue clouds of
tears covering my eyes
out of the clouds I saw grandma
she walked toward me singing
a lullaby
come she whispered let's get
away from the pain let's take a walk
then she nodded her head
and we were gone

"Pain Street" by Clarice tells of pain that is unbearable, incomprehensible, and never-ending. Not being able to feel safe at home or on the streets is horrible for anyone to experience.

I end this section with this piece to send a message of awareness to all readers. We as young women of color experience pain and sorrow on many levels. I hope that some day women of color will not have to share such pain because it will not exist. Until then, we need to come together and offer each other the help and support we need.

PAIN STREET

Clarice Lewis, 17

BLACK

Walking this long street of pain
Mommy screaming, Daddy raping me
Oh brother dear, known of
His great ability to sell the crack heads
Still walking, still feeling pain
Guys screaming "shortie" calling out my name
Making me feel ashamed
Is it me, is this pain my fault
Is this just my street
Someone please help me, tell me
Why when it is me coming in to be seen
This job has no vacancies
Why won't you hire me
I know I am a Black young lady
But my qualifications fit
Ain't this some shit
I guess I am walking this long street
Still walking still feeling pain
Walking down pain street.

RECLAIMING OUR VOICES

Reclaiming Our Voices is all about empowerment. It's about sisters of color recognizing that our voices need to be heard, and speaking out with uplifting strength.

In this section you'll find true feelings and positive messages. You'll find pride, achievement, strength, courage, nature, beauty—and stars. These pieces of writing are honest and inspiring, and they help fulfill the need for connection we all share.

As this book's final section, Reclaiming Our Voices stresses the importance of togetherness and the significance of sisterhood. We hereby reclaim our voices—individually and as one.

Some of my favorite memories have to do with stars. I remember when I was younger, lying on the ground with my mother and looking at the stars in the sky. We would talk and she would hold me. It was almost as if the world was so big but for that time and moment we were the only two who existed.

I also remember lying on the dock at camp looking at the stars with my best friend. We stayed up late talking and staring at the stars, thinking about our future. I remember lying under the stars with another friend as we shared one of the most dramatic, emotional, and close nights of our lives.

When I look at the stars, I am no longer consumed with the problems of everyday life, but instead I think about myself in relation to others. I think about how small I really am in this universe and how my problems are minuscule. When I look at the stars I feel closer to nature and myself, and almost as if I am connected to everybody else who is looking at those same stars—and to everyone else throughout the history of the planet who has gazed in wonder at the night sky.

In "Don't Forget the Stars," Jasmin writes of how looking at the stars can bring us back to reality and make us look truthfully at our own lives. Her piece encourages us to look at our lives in a new way, to appreciate what we have, and to hang on to our sense of hope. The stars have always brought me a sense of peace and tranquility; I hope everyone finds ways in which to achieve these things.

DON'T FORGET THE STARS

Jasmin Kolu Zazaboi, 12
LIBERIAN / EUROPEAN AMERICAN

We think we've felt the worst of it
We think we know it all,
We think our whole lives are built in small black worlds,
Desolate,
And lonely,
We think.
Are we so numb,
So detached,
That we can no longer tell the difference between imagination
    and reality?
Have we forgotten to look up,
Forgotten to see,
The stars that burn so brightly
In our little black imaginary worlds
Have we forgotten,
The existence of happiness
And joy?
Have we forgotten?
Yes I will agree that *sometimes* the world is cruel,

Mean,
Even evil,
Sometimes life is hard,
But look, friend
See the stars?
Count them,
Keep them,
Cherish them,
Remember them,
Don't forget the Stars.

My hair has always been a huge part of my identity, from when I used to straighten it to make it look like my blond friends', to now, the way I let it be itself, curly and nappy. When I cut my hair short in tenth grade and wore it curly, I felt incredibly free. I no longer carried the constraints of assimilation on my head.

I still wear my hair natural and love it. I think Shimere feels the same way.

MY HAIR

Shimere Etheridge, 14
AFRICAN AMERICAN

Masses of tangled frizz line my head
Worn with age and using
Surviving through burn and tear
My hair knotted and uncontrollable

Tangled

Messy

Accepting me as I accept it

Tied

Twisted

Rolled in a bun

Ponytails

Pigtails

Braids

It loves the smell of fresh shampoo

And speaks to me with wisdom and advice

My hair like rope is old and beautiful

Nappy

And wanted

"Me" is the perfect example of what Reclaiming Our Voices is about: strength and overcoming obstacles. Sandra's piece shows a strong sista who once thought the world was safe and has discovered that it's not. However, she is not letting this stop her. She loves herself, rings and all, and as she becomes older she will continue to grow, change, and hopefully inspire others to reclaim their own voices.

ME

Sandra Manzanares, 14

HISPANIC/BLACK

My heart, soul, brain, persona, eyes, smile, hair, skin—it's all me. It's what makes me. I'm unique. I am a Hispanic girl, with both white and black family. Growing up in a predominantly white town isn't always easy. People tend to see the black pigment of your skin before they get to know you. I've always been very social and throughout my years in school I have accomplished the task of becoming friends with mostly everyone. Despite my friendships, I have found myself many times feeling left out. Spending a great deal of time trying to fit in with both the blacks and the whites, it becomes difficult for me to develop my own identity and be secure with it.

When I was younger, I wore very large, flashy rings. One day, my friend was trying to describe me to a person and that person asked if I was the ring lady. Considering that it had been more than a year and a half since I'd worn them, I was surprised. She complimented me on my rings and was disappointed to find that I no longer wore them. She showed me that I was unique, and that others noticed that when I wore the rings. Wearing flashy rings allowed me to be noticed and not blend into the crowd. In a way, the flashy rings are like my skin color, allowing me to be noticed, especially when I am with my white friends.

In my school, there is a bit of segregation. At lunch the preppies, the jocks, the freaks, the geeks, the popular and those who wish to be, and then the blacks and whites sit mostly separate from one another, forming their own cliques. In this town, a crowd of blacks can stand out like a lightbulb in the dark. And most of them do tend to hang out together.

In school, I find times where I don't feel that I fit in anywhere. I'm not white enough to fit in with all my white friends and not black enough to fit in with all my black friends. During the teenage years, when fitting in is a primary goal, it's frustrating to feel that you are not fully accepted by a certain type of people.

My assumption was that racism only existed a long time ago. Well, I was wrong. I became angry to find that many people talk about the black community as a whole, as if we were all one thing. I once heard some girls talking about how *they* can do such cool things with their feet when dancing. The "they" referred to black people. It was as if we were not to be spoken of. Much of the tension that exists between the black and white communities is due to careless comments that disregard the feelings of others. It's sad to see not many of my race participate in some of the sports and music activities that I do. Sometimes it almost seems as if everyone else knows a secret that I'm not being told. I am very proud of my heritage. I admit, sometimes I wonder if it would be better if we were all blue-eyed and blond. But that would not make *me* unique. I wouldn't be able to be tan all year round, my hair might not look as cute with braids, and I wouldn't be able to dance salsa as skillfully. I just wouldn't be me. I like the person I am, and I'm proud of both my black and my white heritage.

My life has meaning, as everyone's should, and once we realize where we stand, we can understand that meaning. It takes much empowerment to be who you really are, and I don't feel that I have fully accomplished that as of now. I'm definitely confident with who I am and what I believe, but I have yet to encounter the effects of peer pressure. I realize that I can stand alone, that I can be myself, and that others will respect me for who I am.

Now, as I grow to be a young adult, I realize that the world isn't sugar coated as it appeared to me as a child. People are sometimes treated differently because of the color of their skin, but if we can get past that, we will be better off. I love myself, everything about me. I have flaws, we all do. I accept every part of myself—the good and the bad. I will always be me. I am unique, skin and all.

*W*riting enables me to be me. Nothing more.

I don't have to get dressed up or wear makeup. I can just sit down and type. It's as if my hand and my mind are one. The words are slowly formed onto the computer screen or into a notebook, telling me how I am feeling or what is going on.

My writing is not about showing off or impressing others. It is strictly about my self. I think Alicia feels the same. In "Rhythmic Vibrations," she tells of what her writing means to her. I hope all you sisters of color who write can feel the same vibrations as she and I do. It's a wonderful feeling.

RHYTHMIC VIBRATIONS

Alicia Rodrigo, 14
AFRICAN AMERICAN / HISPANIC

My writing is a release of love, hatred, passion, desire, and
  revenge
It is a way for the hard emotions spiraling down the never-ending
  tunnel, which is my mind to be expressed and articulated on
  paper
The ever so elegant yet powerful combinations of syllables and
  rhymes dance on my tongue, ready to be released into harsh-
  ness of the world
Vibrating through my body and finally being released in patterns
  on my paper
Representing the intricate weaving designs of my heart, my soul,
  and my mind
What if no one is watching? It wouldn't make a difference
  because my words are mine
My words are me

I swallow the words and they become part of me
I then release them through my pores to be explored and shared
  with the world
I don't gobble the feelings like a monster, I inhale them as I would
  inhale the delicate and intriguing smell of incense and smoke
I don't have to worry about the impressions my writing gives
I'm not trying to impress anyone but me.

I have yet to hear a white person talk about how beautiful his or her skin is. Not that they shouldn't, because if they feel that it is so much a part of them, then they should. However, I cannot tell you how many pieces I received from girls of color that focus solely on skin. They described the deep tones, the light shades, and the feelings that accompany skin color. Focusing on skin color is something that comes to us naturally. Because we are so often judged on our skin color, it's an important part of our identity. And in order to counteract the negative effects we encounter every day, we turn our skin into something beautiful, something we are proud of, and something we want to write about.

BROWN SKIN

Joycelyn Hubbard, 15
AFRICAN AMERICAN

Deep mahogany
Melanin skin

God's sunscreen
All wrapped within

A sweeter berry
Purple gums
And a milky white smile
Smooth lavender skin

Rich browns
Even darker
In the sun
Daring gaze

All wrapped within

Both Leslie and Melanie wrote about personal obstacles they have overcome. They both write in the third person, as though they wanted to distance themselves from the experiences they describe.

Overcoming obstacles is something we can all be proud of. Whether it is tackling a subject in school that is hard or recovering from physical abuse, when we achieve something, we should take notice. We should also be proud of one another for the accomplishments we all make. I would like to say not only thank you but also that I am very proud of Leslie and Melanie.

GIRL WHO

Melanie Medina, 18
PUERTO RICAN AMERICAN

Girl who is not happy.
Girl who had been raped by her father.
Girl who had kids—young age.
Girl who didn't know how to read and write.
Girl who didn't know her ABC's.
Girl who had HIV.
Girl who didn't give up her life.
Girl who pushed so hard for her life and kids.
Everything she did for her life; was not easy.
But she passes her GED and gets a job.
Now girl who has HIV wants to love herself more.

THE GIRL I KNEW

Leslie Neyland, 15
AFRICAN AMERICAN

 I once knew a girl with a secret. She hid behind a disguise of smiles and only opened up when she was alone in the darkness. Paranoia enabled her to believe that everyone was curious about her or knew pieces of her secret. Her worst fear was having the sheet pulled off, revealing her secret to everyone. She thought people would shun her if they knew; never letting another person get close enough to see.

I once knew a girl who was shy. It was hard for her to look a person in the eyes, and meeting new people was a fear. She was soft-spoken and said as little as possible. When she was in the privacy of her own home and with familiar faces of her family, she could talk for hours; never allowing herself to get to know new people.

I once knew a girl with low self-esteem. She constantly put herself down and never felt she was good enough. Her feelings restrained her from dreaming, and she hid herself in her own world, never opening up to another soul.

I once knew a girl who was competitive. All she ever wanted was to win and being first was all she knew. Her worst fear was losing and her whole life was a competition. She walked around all day wearing her game face and only had time to practice. She would let no one get in her way, never having time to make friends, only rivals.

I once knew a girl who was vain. Her mirror was her favorite companion and bragging was a hobby. She looked down at people and carried herself with a flawless cape. She thought everyone was either envious or they looked up to her, never finding a person she could relate to.

A real friend revealed to her the way others truly felt about her attitude.

She talked to her school counselor about her past. She helped her cope and realize that she had no reason to be ashamed or hide.

She lost that race but her father told her she was still his winner and that he loved her.

She found that she was good at new things, and her mother told her she was proud of her.

I now know a girl who has nothing to hide.

I now know a girl with high self-esteem.

I now know a girl with plenty of pride.

I now know a girl who is confident.

I now know a girl who believes that achieving her best is the best, and that her past is where it belongs . . . in the past or left behind.

Neftara is a poet, a philosopher, and an educator. Her beautiful piece shows intelligence and the ability to capture and describe the world around us with beauty and passion.

"Essence of Life" speaks to us of water and its place in nature and in our lives. I believe that nature is an essential part of spirituality. Tribal people of all continents have a deep understanding of nature, which shapes their spiritual lives.

It seems as though Neftara has reached a kind of balancing point in her life. She is able to see the beauty and power of the earth, nature, and the elements, and how they affect our lives.

Thank you so much for your poem and your beautiful insights, Neftara.

ESSENCE OF LIFE

Neftara O. Clark, 18

BLACK

 Such a magnificent yet mysterious force within our Mother/Father God's natural landscapes.

So humble in its quiet presence, yet so aggressive in its demeanor and ability to

Demand respect from even the biggest of creatures.

Ripples of wetness flowing so smoothly and effortlessly across the mounds that encompass the walls of the world.

A warming and nurturing substance that breathes life into the very essence that makes human beings' existence possible.

A protective shield that not only acts like a collective guardian to all of the life-forms that exist beneath its wavy arms, it also has a welcoming rapport with

Those life forces and forms existing outside the walls of its misty folds.

A wonderfully calming source of energy with the amazing ability to move through the body, offering a sense of renewal to tired muscles and nutrients to strained nerves, while revitalizing the spiritual being and cleansing the physical body of toxins.

A sensual and important element within the world that refreshes the very vessels that allow man and woman to create and sustain life.

An ancient storyteller, carrying the souls of our foremothers and forefathers, who transitioned during the middle passage, forever replaying the voices of pain, anguish, and despair through the magnificent windows of crystal mist.

Cascading sounds of security, patience, strength, birth, cleansing, energy, calmness, and power—LIFE radiating from the warm embrace as it gracefully

Flows over the world's rocky cliffs and mountains, becoming a symbolic beacon of light and hope, infusing man's and woman's internal and external being with the necessary essentials to expand LIFE!!!!

Water: something we must come to understand, preserve, and become one with, for without it, there would truly be no US, WE, HE, nor SHE, for it is our Mother, it is our Father, it is our Creator, it is our Sustainer, and it is our Maintainer, it's . . . it is . . . it is . . .

It is the very Essence of Life.

My name is a huge part of my identity. When I was five, I wanted my name to be Ramona after the girl in the children's books. As I grew older I wanted to change it to Megan or Jennifer because that's what all the popular girls were named. Then there was the time when I wanted a really bizarre name that no one could pronounce because for some reason I was sure they would all think I was really cool.

Then I began to love my own name. I loved the sound, the simplicity, and all the meanings. My name began to mean more to me than just something I was called; it began to be my identity.

Ebony's search for her name seemed more like a search for identity. As Ebony and I both learned about our names, we both seemed to learn more about ourselves. I'm glad Ebony found what she was looking for.

CHASING EBONY

Ebony L. Herron, 19
AFRICAN AMERICAN

"Knowledge of the self is the mother of all knowledge. So it is incumbent on me to know myself, to know it completely, to know its minutiae, its characteristics, its subtleties, and its very atoms."

Khalil Gibran, *The Philosophy of Logic*

Treace. Treace. Tree-cee. Latraice. Ebony. Eb-o-nee. Eb-nee. Ebany. Ebony. Herron. Har-ron. Her-on. Har-in. Ebony Latraice Herron. Me.

I remember feeling not quite like a Treace. I wondered how I came to be called that. I needed to know why they called me that. It didn't seem to identify anything extraordinary or peculiar about me like the nicknames given to my cousins Red, Beena, Byrd, Junebug, Stone, or Bid Daddy and Little Daddy, Big Twin and Little Twin, Ladybug, Mop, or even Doo-Doo. It was impressive that someone would take the time to give you a nickname or to accidentally give you one. Ones like those special pet names shared only between two people that eventually rings from the throats of all your friends and relatives.

I asked my mother why. "It comes from your middle name," she explained. "But my middle name is Latraice (pronounced 'trese') not Latreace ('tree-C')," I said basically to myself. Where did the "e" sound at the end come from? It seemed to be added for style, I thought. There was still no connection between the name and me. The chase continued.

No sooner had I begun my name crisis than I received a moniker of damnation. It was during the time we lived in a housing project. My aunt and her five children lived in an adjacent row in the third house. Most of my time was spent over there. As an only child, I loved my cousins. There were four older boys and one baby girl; I was in the middle. But I was different from all of my cousins. They all had brothers and/or sisters, and had to share and wear hand-me-downs, and had limited Christmas gifts. Whereas I was *spoiled*.

I didn't exactly know why they damned me with that name, but I knew it had something to do with their having seen *The Wizard of Oz*. Under circumstances I don't remember, I found myself enclosed and sealed in a box that was the intertwining of big and little black arms that taunted me. "Wikketty, Wikketty, Witch of the West! Wickketty, Wickketty Witch!" was their ceaseless chant. Over and over and over it rang from the depths of their cruel souls until I cried and cried and cried. I don't recall what month or year they decided to grant me my freedom, but I know I was glad. I didn't fully comprehend why they did it until I recalled a conversation I had with my grandmother. They were jealous of me. And in the midst of all that they crafted that name for me. Nothing loving, cute, or special about it.

I began chasing my own nicknames. Cornflake. Suga. Candy. Cookie. (I liked junk food.) Skip. Gem. Rainbow Bright. Strawberry Shortcake. (I idolized them.) Babygirl. Well, it was a start! When I was about ten, an older girl told me that I was always smiling. She said that every time she saw me I was grinning long and wide. She told me that she was going to call me "Kool-Aid." There was no denying, from that point on, I outdid the Kool-Aid Man.

I was called Ebony in school. The name rolled over me like water on a duck. I never acknowledged it as me. There was no bond; in fact, it didn't feel as if it even belonged to me. It became even more estranged from me when I got to high school. The name Ebony appeared to belong to so many girls. I even met a boy once named Ebony. Gross! More so, I've come across white girls with the name. Unbelievable! I also thought my family was the only one with Herron as a last name. I was at a serious loss.

I initiated a personalization of my name. I searched the dictionary and found ebony. Ebony was a beautiful black wood yielded from a tree in Africa. Herron was in there, too, minus an "r." It was close enough for me to feel I had a little more than the average person did, since my first and last names were in the dictionary. I began to experiment with variations of Ebony and my "cool and hip" status. I called myself Eb-god and Eb. I wrote it on folders, walls, desks, my pant legs, and even the bottoms of my shoes. I would stand in the mirror and recite my first name, middle name, and last name separately, and then all together. I would ask my reflection, "Who is Ebony Latraice Herron?" I incorporated role-playing. I introduced myself to various people and held conversations with them. I took note of my countenance and attitude as I said my name. This became a ritual for me. It was a transformation.

I became my name and my name became me. We were one. When I looked in the mirror I saw Ebony. Not just a face that belonged to the name. I was Ebony Latraice Herron. I am she. Beautiful, special, and unique. I also came to realize that my nickname Treace was indeed special, assigned to me by my mother who to this day refers to me by the name. I found a connection and the chase was over.

Diomara's poem touches on the surviving and fighting attitude of girls of color. Together we all seem to put up with so much, but inside we seem to know who we really are. As the poem starts off it is only Diomara, but as it progresses it includes all of us.

UNTITLED

Diomara Chaparro, 16
PUERTO RICAN

Sometimes I felt I was imprisoned inside of me.
I was scared to cry because they'll think that I was weak,
Sometimes scared to express my feelings because they won't
    understand me.
I was never like every other child,
I was always alone and quiet, I never let anyone even try to get
    close to me, because I was scared of what they thought or what
    they might have said.
But I couldn't hold it anymore.
I needed to break out of my prison.
So I broke loose.
No one could have told me that I wasn't smart enough,
Skinny enough, strong enough.
I blew off my mind.
I'm the same as all of you,
I have the same figure, the same intelligence and even maybe
More morals.
I was always taught not to discriminate because of sex, color, race
    or stature in life,
Yet everyone wants to discriminate me, judge me,

And undermine my intelligence.
But no matter how they see me
I know who I really am, and no matter how hard
They try to make us seem different
We will always be equal
In the eyes of truth.

In my sophomore year of high school I started a group for students of color. The group was meant to allow for us to discuss our problems, concerns, happiness, and whatever else was on our minds as kids of color. As the idea came out to the high school I received a great deal of negativity. Many of the white kids felt betrayed and left out, and the kids of color felt that if they joined they would be racist.

I continually reiterated the fact that there was nothing wrong with what we were doing and the group was a support group, not a racist group. As the first meeting began the room was full. I was ecstatic to see so many faces, especially from kids who were excited and wanted to participate. Once the meeting started, though, I began to sense some hesitation. One kid constantly interrupted and tried numerous times to take over the group. I realized that his rudeness was a result of his being uncomfortable. Instead of voicing this, he tried to make fun of or interrupt me. I was very insulted, but I realized his actions were not aimed at me. He was fighting the fact that although he wanted to participate in the meeting, he did not want to make the white kids angry. He was treating me badly as a way to pretend he did not want to be there and was in a sense baiting me to kick him out.

After I realized this and stopped feeling hurt, I was thankful for what had happened. Although I felt bad for the way this boy had treated me, I realized his anger was misguided. He had taken it out on the wrong person, and even though I was hurt, we both learned from the experience and later talked about it.

Deymis's story is similar to mine. She was verbally violated by another person of color for merely being with the people she was with. She then learned from the experience, and it has now helped her in life. So often I think we as people of color wrongfully attack one another and instead should focus our anger other places. In my case I was lucky enough to sit down with the kid who had been rude to me, and together we found the source of his anger. I hope someday Deymis can sit down with the person who was rude to her and find out the true source of her anger.

WHAT MADE ME STRONGER

Deymis Baquero, 16
PUERTO RICAN

One thing that I never thought I was going to experience firsthand was racism and prejudice from another person. I never imagined that I would have to go through it and that it would pain and anger me as much as it did. During the incident I thought I would remain angry and think about hating the person. Instead I thank God for the situation because it helped me understand many things about other people as well as myself.

It began during my freshman year in high school. I had my crowd of friends, just like everyone else did. My friends, coincidentally, were all Puerto Rican, but any other race was welcome to be a part of our circle. When the New Year began, I started to have problems with a young lady in my grade who disliked me greatly, but did not say why. As time went by the reasons gradually changed. First it was because I had long hair and nails, next it was because I was dating a guy that most of the girls liked, but then the last reason became apparent in a very uncomfortable way. She and I had our eighth-period class together. She entered the class and saw my friends and me talking, and said, "Why don't all of you spics shut up already, you talk too much." This was very surprising coming from a female minority just like me. I felt that we needed to unite, not work against each other.

I wondered why these things happen and why it had happened to me. When it was all over, I thought, Why am I making this a tragedy? I'm going to use this to learn something. I learned many things about my emotional position, my maturity as a female, my anger level, and my self-confidence. Emotionally, I learned that I am overly sensitive and that I need to control that. My sensitivity makes me lose my strength, which is something that I don't want to do. Strength is the key to survival and survival is the key to life. My maturity was put to a very difficult test at this point. How far would I go with the situation? I proved that I am a very controlled person. I personally felt that I handled the situation well, even though my anger level went through the roof because I take great pride in my nationality. My self-confidence became even higher than before, because I realized that I should love my background and myself even more than I already did.

The summer of 2001 I went to a Jill Scott concert. She was awesome. She not only sang beautifully, but she also spoke about interesting and important issues. For a long time afterward I thought of her as the ultimate. I mean, she was it. The splendor, grace, magnificence, and talent that she brought to the stage proved to me that women of color made it, and did it with style. When I got home, I began to read some pieces for the book. I realized that as awesome as Jill Scott is, so is each one of us. We have that talent, knowledge, and beauty.

In her poem, Candice lets us know just how exquisite she is, and in turn how tremendous we are also.

UNTITLED

Candice J. Bingham, 18
AFRICAN AMERICAN

I am beautiful
As sensual as the midnight rain nourishing the soul
I am the earth
I am dark, mystical, mysterious
Like the dark side of the moon
Nature conforms to my cycle
I walk with the pride of a lioness surveying her queendom
Such rhythm
Grace that of a swan sliding across the water
I am deep, a genius, a seductress
Like the ocean floor
I speak in proverb and verse
My words are filled with the infinite wisdom of old
I am the divine universal life force of the cosmos
I breathe life into all creation
My very breath making greener the grass
And brighter the sun
I bear the energy of enlightenment
My eyes are the window to the motherland
My glorious crown of wooly hair
Signals the very ethers of space
My spirit illuminates all I may touch
It soars through the cerulean sky to the firmament
Like a wild bird
My voice resonates, piercing your very soul
Reducing you to peasantry
My voluptuous body
The curves aligned with the silhouette of God

As fertile as the crop circle
As majestic as Mt. Kilimanjaro
As rich as gold
As sweet as a fragrance of a silk rose
I am mother of all mankind

My stepfather often speaks of finding links to our lands of origin. Finally I have begun to understand what he is saying. He is referring to the bond that connects people to their own land. He told me how he, as a Native American, feels as he sees nature, spirits, and beauty interwoven and interconnected, here in his own land.

I wondered how I would feel if I were actually to go to where my ancestors are from. Would I be strongly connected to Trinidad or Romania or England or Africa? Or would I feel the same as I do in the United States? Then I began to think about maybe not feeling connected to that land but to that history. I may never feel at one with the land where I once belonged, but I will always try to maintain the heritage and history that evolved on that land. I will never forget my roots, and by doing so I am acknowledging, fighting for, and thanking all those who came before me.

In "Daughter of Africa," Jeanette speaks of how she is a woman of Africa and carries that history with her. She reminds us all of the links we have with our own land. Whether we are there or not, we are a part of it. She also speaks about carrying on the legacy of black women and how we should never forget or deny where we are from. We should all be thankful and appreciative of where we come from and use it as a source of pride to lift up not only ourselves but also those who surround us.

DAUGHTER OF AFRICA

Jeanette Asabere, 16
AFRICAN (GHANAIAN) AMERICAN

In me are the past, the present, and the future. By looking at me you can judge me by your perceptions, your thoughts, and your feelings. Many things can be going through your head at this moment. Some who may know me well may think they know me, still many of you are wondering what I hold and possess. You may think of me as weird, ugly, beautiful, or awkward, but did you know that I am the daughter of Africa?

No, you did not know. You did not know that my ancestors walked upon the continent of Africa. Their heads held high with their glowing ebony skin darkened by the sun. Their dark penetrating eyes that sparkled in the sunlight. The women with their hair shaven low due to the unmanageability of the conditions of the climate. Thick, nappy, yet looked beautiful and unique with African style. Kente cloth wrapped around them, some with babies tied in the back. Thick and round, short and skinny these women were. Their hands smooth and rough showed the effects of hard work in the farms, planting yams and picking plantains. From these women I get my rough, smooth hands, my piercing eyes, my dark skin.

I soon became the woman of the '60s, '70s, and '80s; discriminated upon yet still holding on to that unique African style. Whether with braids; pressed, pomaded hair; my puffed and soft Afro; high-heeled shoes; or big earrings, I created a different style. Yet as I come to evolve I still hold on to my African heritage, my rough hands. My integrity, my dignity, my pride of being black. I am the future, holding on to what was handed down. I cannot deny it or overlook it because no matter what, it will always be there. Always that constant reminder that black is beautiful.

Sunny's poem is awesome. The thing I like most about it is the way it symbol-izes us, sisters of color. We are all beautiful flowers that can blossom and thrive no matter where we are planted. We are everlasting in a world that may not accept us, but cannot deny our strength and splendor.

Untitled

Sunny Rasmussen, 18

LAC DU FLAMBEAU AND BAD RIVER OJIBWE

no matter where it is
or what surrounds it,
a flower will bloom.
because that is what it does
all different, all perfect,
all beautiful.
a flower,
it is a constant
in an ever changing
world.

When I first began writing this book I was scared. I was afraid that people wouldn't like it or that they wouldn't agree with it, but most of all I was scared that I would get the all too common, "What do you know, you're hardly even black." I was worried that my light skin, my family, and the way in which

I act and speak would give people the impression that I don't really know what being a person of color is all about. I spoke to my mother, my friends, and many others about this fear. I did not want to be known as the girl who compiled pieces of writing for girls of color but who had no idea what it was like. Then I began to think about how being of color is usually described. I began to realize that being of color does not mean that I was raised in the ghetto. It does not mean that I spend all my time with people of my race or that I speak in a certain dialect. Being of color is who I am, and who I will always be. I am strong because of it, and I am very proud of it. Nobody can tell me I do not know the struggle or that I am less of color because no one is me. I am a strong, intelligent, beautiful woman of color.

In "The Struggle: Black, Light-skinned, and Smart," Candice writes of how she felt growing up and being picked on simply for being the way she is. Because Candice has light skin and was placed in higher classes, she was forced to confront depression, intimidation, and the real meaning of being black.

THE STRUGGLE: BLACK, LIGHT-SKINNED, AND SMART

Candice Fleming, 16

BLACK

It first started when I was in the sixth grade. The name calling, the threats, the verbal abuse. They called me names like "wigger" or "cracker," "Uncle Tom" and "sellout." I came home every night, trying to understand why I wasn't black enough. I hated myself. I hated my light, tan skin, and my honey-colored hair, and my light brown eyes. I hated that I was smart and was placed in classes with whites, who were my only friends. My mother was worried that I would never make any Black friends. Why should I be friends with those who wouldn't even try and get to know me? Why should I be friends with those who would threaten me with bodily harm every time I made honor roll, or laughed every time I tried to introduce myself to them? Why bother? My dad always said not to worry, because I would go to a good school, get married, and live happily ever after. I didn't care about happily ever after or going to a good school.

I just wanted them to be my friends.

I am a very outgoing and friendly person, and I had many good friends that I could count on. I understood, for the most part, that everyone was not always going to like me. But an entire race of females was something I couldn't accept. Their words cut like sharp knives into my self-esteem, and I began to sink deeper into a depression that swallowed me like a black hole. My grades began to fall and I became shy . . . no, frightened of my own race—frightened of those who were supposed to be my sisters. I sat at lunch and had half-eaten oranges thrown on my head. I ran to the bathroom and cried, only to have them torment me in there. I watched my little sister grow into a bitter and unforgiving person, tormented by the little sisters of the same girls who had convinced me that I was a disgrace—a joke. I began to hate. My heart grew cold, and I no longer cared about myself, or those who cared about me. I wanted to die.

And I almost did take my life, which was worth less to me than the spit they hurled at my head. I almost became the person they wanted me to be: cold, bitter, and selfish. Until I realized that the problem didn't lie within me, or within an entire race of women. I realized that when they chided me for being intelligent, and for my friendliness, that they were making the stereotypical loud, angry, and unintelligent black woman a reality. By refusing to get to know me and accept me for who I was, they were showing me that they were scared of reaching out, scared of exploring new ideas, scared of being a "sellout."

I was determined not to be afraid. I was determined to show the world an intelligent, courteous, friendly and beautiful Black woman. I began to understand that I didn't have to prove my Blackness to anyone. Being Black is already a part of me, and my heritage is something that no amount of teasing and torment could take from me. I was determined not to deprive myself of the privilege of meeting new people because of the color of their skin, the way they spoke, their physical disability, or mental handicap. I was determined to make my parents proud of me . . . to make *me* proud of me. To be the hero of my own story, which is ongoing and undulating with highs and lows. And I think—with God's help and the help of some very special people in my life—that I am becoming that hero.

As I grew older, I made new friends—both Black and other races—who would surround me in a circle of acceptance and love, and appreciate me for who I am. I am involved in church and school activities that allow me to further explore and appreciate my heritage. I am very active in sports and singing. I am watching my sister grow into a beautiful young lady. I love myself and I love my life.

I wrote this not out of anger or resentment. I wrote this for any young person who experienced what I went through. I wrote this to tell them that they are loved and children of God, and He will never leave them or forsake them. I wrote this to tell them to never change who they are and to keep an open mind and a strong heart. I wrote this to say thank you to all of those who helped me realize that my life was worthwhile and that many people love me. I wrote this to cleanse my heart once more, and to show everyone reading this compilation that I bear no hatred . . . only love. And love is all I need.

For Elise—I love you.

Now is the time that we should come together. We should learn from each other, learn from our past and learn how to successfully construct our future. We are women of color and it is our time. We are all intelligent. And by supporting, loving, nurturing, believing in, and empowering one another we can become a strong force and overcome many obstacles.

FOR SO LONG

Janelle Camille Cates, 16
BLACK

For so long
    We been held down
    Told to sit down and
    Told to slow down.
For so long
    We been held up
    Beat up
    Locked up and
    Told to shut up.
For so long
    We've been oppressed
    Depressed and
    Stressed.
But now it is OUR TIME!

Time to
    Get up
    Stand up and
    Speak up.
Time to
    Go
    Don't take no mo'.
We will continue the struggle.
Now's the time to give OUR BEST.

When I first received this poem, I just sat and smiled. I loved it. I absolutely loved it. In so few lines, it explained what I wanted to get across to every girl. The purpose of this book was not to create anger but instead to draw connections, not to promote separation but instead to find commonalities. Kristin says everything I want to in these lines, and it is the perfect way to end this book. Thank you to all the girls; I hope you will all sing soft to me, because I will always listen, and I hope that you will also.

UNTITLED

Kristin Soong, 17

BIRACIAL

Sing Soft to me, Sweet Sister,
You know not what you do.
Your words divulge to me, a listener,
This world's contempt for you.

Sing Soft to me, Sweet Sister,
Your time is waning here.
As voice subsides to placid whisper,
Just know that I am near.

Acknowledgments

Before even beginning to show gratitude to anyone else, I need to send my praise, admiration, and thanks to all the girls of color who submitted pieces. I appreciate and love every piece I received, and I truly wish I could have included them all. Thank you to all the girls who supported me, believed in me, and told me so. The letters I received not only kept me going but also provided a sense of strength within me that I hope I've shown throughout these pages. Thank you all; none of this could have happened without you.

Thank you, also, to the many teachers, counselors, mentors, volunteers, and friends who urged girls of color to write for this book.

Agnes Birnbaum of Bleecker Street Associates welcomed my idea and helped me make it come true. Agnes became not only my agent but also a family friend and a wonderful support person.

Deb Brody at Henry Holt and Company helped me not only by editing but also by having faith in me and trusting me to deliver a strong and captivating manuscript.

Individuals throughout my life have also helped me with this book. First and foremost, I need to thank my mother. Without her encouragement, love, hope, knowledge, and support this book would never exist. She has helped me to know not only who I am but how I relate to others and also how to put that into words. I cannot ever repay her for all that she has given me, and I hope someday I am able to show her just how much that has been.

My stepfather, Mike, has also been a strong influence in my life.

His teachings and role modeling in social activism have helped me develop the passion and ability to fight strongly for what I believe in.

My siblings, Mica and Mato, I thank you both so much. For all the times I was interrupted, yelled at, and tickled while writing, I owe you. You both helped me keep my sanity and remember that one of my most important roles is as a big sister.

My extended family has also supported me and cherished me during the writing of this book. Without the love, truth, and admiration of my grandparents I would not know the strong roots and love that I come from. I would also not know the true meaning of happiness and laughter without my grandfather's fake cell phone and my grandmother's singing of "Happy Birthday" on our voicemail. I also owe a great deal to my aunt Victoria, uncle Paul, and my cousins, Grace, Emily, and Nicholas. To my extended stepfamily I also owe gratitude: Delores, Robert, Tim, Yolanda, and Joseph, I thank you all for making me laugh and supporting me.

As the book came together I received and continue to receive a great deal of support from numerous agencies and organizations. I would like to thank Gene Batiste and the rest of NAIS (National Association of Independent Schools). Gene has been a friend, a teacher, and a guiding light in helping me with personal decisions and trusting me. Thanks to all of NCCJ (National Conference for Community and Justice) for instilling in me a longing for equality and an ability to use the right actions, words, and ways to achieve it. Jarrod Schwartz and Shannelle Henry were not only helpful in my search for self but also supported me and helped me find my voice. My gratitude also goes to Kinkos for staying open 24/7; to Joe Osborn for helping provide stability to our family while this book was written; to Paul Heckel for his excellent design work; and to AvailAbility for typing and working very fast.

Great teachers have without a doubt helped mold me into who I am today. Many of my teachers have believed in me and supported me wonderfully throughout the writing of this book. Most importantly, I need to thank Charisse Jackson. What started out as a one-hour class helped develop a wonderful bond and create an awesome friendship. She has trusted me, loved me, listened to me, and cared for me as no one else can. Marjie Butler, Armond Lawson, David Drinkard, and Thomas Lubeck have also been wonderful teachers who have cared and taught me not only the basics of school but also important life lessons.

My friends and allies deserve a great deal of recognition. Alice: I love you and know that we will be best friends far into the future. Carrie: You are a model feminist and a wonderful ally. Genevieve: HOLEYBUCKETS, I love ya! Skyler: You have taught me a great deal about life, I love you. Sarah: You have always made me laugh, please don't forget, go "D" team. Helena and Stacey: Your support has been a huge help. Courtney and Alana: thanks for helping me stay sane. Kenny: Your impact on me is more than you could ever know. Go Ike! Mallory: You're beautiful. Kazia, Emily S., and Alix: as you have all paved the way, it has been much easier to follow in your footsteps. Daryl: Eve says hey. To the McIntyre, Sanderson/Randall, Gamble, Prunty, and Jackson families: I thank you all for taking me into your homes and treating me as if I were a member of the family. To the participants in Anytowns and DRs throughout all time: You have established a community in which I feel comfortable and appreciated—thanks.

Without the powerful influences of my heroines and heroes I would not be at all where I am today. I thank Maxine Waters, Farai Chideya, M. Rose Barkley, Maya Angelou, Toi Derricotte, Nikki Giovanni, and Oprah Winfrey for their inspiration. Also my appreciation goes to The Roots, Common, Mos Def, Lauryn Hill, Jill Scott, Erykah Badu, India Arie, Bob Marley, Tribe Called Quest, Outkast, Black Eyed Peas, and DeAngelo for creating positive music with a message.

My yearning for continuing growth and awareness has come from a plethora of influences, both helpful and obstructive. I would like to express gratitude to all the ignorant people who have helped me want to continue to strive for change. Without you, my passion would not be nearly as strong and my anger would not be nearly as fueled. My appreciation goes especially to the school administrators who have presented an incredible amount of resistance to all my ideas for change; to teachers who have pretended to teach their subjects but instead taught ignorance and oppression; and to the parents who wouldn't let their daughters bring a girl of color into their homes. And special thanks go to all those individuals who follow me in stores, call me derogatory and offensive names, and keep me from doing and achieving what I want to do: you all help me stay dedicated to and focused on social change.

About the Author

Iris Jacob is an eighteen-year-old biracial female with a strong commitment to diversity issues. She has been a student facilitator at numerous diversity conferences, has started affinity groups for students of color and women at her high school, and codirected a youth leadership institute addressing topics of oppression, prejudice, and awareness.